THE WOLF PLAYS

THE
WOLF
PLAYS

WOLFBOY &
PROM NIGHT OF
THE LIVING DEAD

by Brad Fraser

Prairie Play Series: 12 • Series Editor, Diane Bessai

Canadian Cataloguing in Publication Data

Fraser, Brad, 1959-
  The wolf plays
  (Prairie play series ; 12)
Contents: Wolfboy. - Prom night of the living dead.
ISBN 0-920897-49-5
  I. Title. II. Title: Wolfboy. III. Title:
Prom night of the living dead. IV. Series.
PS8561.R294W65 1993   C812'.54   C93-090444-3
PR9199.3.F73W65 1993

Printed and bound in Canada by Hignell Printing Limited

NeWest Publishers Limited
#310, 10359-82 Avenue
Edmonton, Alberta
T6E 1Z9

CREDITS
Editors for the Press: Diane Bessai and Don Kerr
Cover design: Brian Huffman
Interior design: Bob Young/BOOKENDS DESIGNWORKS
Cover Photo: Grant Olson
Wolfboy photos: University of Saskatchewan Libraries – 25th Street
    Theatre MSS – I. Seasons.10.1981-82. (vii)Photographs (d)Wolfboy
Financial Assistance: NeWest Press gratefully acknowledges the financial
    assistance of The Canada Council; The Alberta Foundation for the Arts,
    a beneficiary of the Lottery Fund of the Government of Alberta; and The
    NeWest Institute for Western Canadian Studies.

(Prairie Play Series Number 12)

Every effort has been made to obtain permission for photographs. If there is
an omission or error the editors and publisher would be grateful to be so
informed.

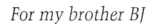

For my brother BJ

OTHER BRAD FRASER PLAYS PUBLISHED BY NEWEST PRESS

The Ugly Man

TABLE OF CONTENTS

■

WOLFBOY

WOLFBOY:

PLAYWRIGHT'S INTRODUCTION

In 1981 I had just written and directed my first produced full length play for Walterdale Theatre, Edmonton's amateur theatre. The title of the play was *Mutants* and I was lucky enough to have it seen by Paul Thompson, then head of Toronto's Theatre Passe Muraille and one of the original creators of that very 1970s theatre form known as the "collective creation." I met with Paul, who was very enthusiastic about my work. He left Edmonton with a promise to pass my work along to anyone he thought might be interested in it.

A few months later – I was working as a directory assistance operator at the time, experimenting with drugs, calling myself a punk, and toying with the idea that perhaps I wasn't bi-sexual as I'd been telling people, but actually gay – when someone named Andy Tahn called from 25th Street Theatre in Saskatoon. Andy was the artistic director of the theatre at the time, and Paul had told him I was an exciting new playwriting voice he should contact. Andy had read *Mutants* (which combined every theatrical possibility/cliché in existence) and wanted to know if I was working on anything new that he might read.

I wasn't. Working shifts, endless socializing and trying to figure out exactly who I was and what I wanted out of life had taken precedence over my budding writing career. However, I knew this opportunity shouldn't be missed, so I lied and told him yes indeed, I was working on a brand new play. He wanted to know what it was about. I quickly (thank God for all those years of improvisational acting training) spun an nonexistent script out of an idea I'd been toying with for some time. That idea was a play about two boys in a mental home. One of these boys is a suicidal jock. The other is a street kid who may or may not be a werewolf. Andy was intrigued and wanted to know how far along I was in the writing. I lied again and told him I'd finished the first act. He wanted to see it immediately. I told him I was busy at the moment and it might be a week or two before I could get the act to him. He said no problem and rang off, having made me promise to get the act to him as soon as possible. The minute I was off the phone I pulled the dust-cover from my Smith Corona portable electric (my very first purchase on my Bay card) and started to write.

One week later Andy received the first act of a play called *Die Lycanthrope*. He called me immediately to say he liked it, they were planning a festival of new plays in their 1981/82 season and did I think I could have the play completed for December so they might consider it for the festival in the new year. Absolutely, I replied ecstatically. After all, it was only July and December was a long way off. Finishing the script would be no problem. I spent August working on the second act of what I was quickly discovering would be a three-act play. I sent act two to Andy and he called back with great enthusiasm. They loved the script and wanted to purchase the rights to produce the play without having seen the third act. No problem. They telegramed (this is pre-fax) a contract, which I signed without even really reading, and all was set. I had just turned 22 and my first professional production was set for the following year. I could see everything falling into place. The show, which I considered brilliant, would be a huge hit. It would take Saskatoon by storm, open to ecstatic reviews, be produced everywhere else in Canada and finally open in New York. I knew I was destined to be a world famous playwright before my twenty-third birthday. And I hadn't even completed the third act. Not that I was worried. There was plenty of time.

Then things changed.

The new play festival idea fell through for some reason I can't recall and maybe never knew. 25th Street had to shuffle its season and I got a call asking me if I could have the show ready for October. October? No problem. How hard could it be to write a third act? I was brilliant. I could do anything. Just give me a little time to think about it.

But the third act wasn't coming all that easy. I spent hours on my headset at Edmonton Telephones, half-heartedly giving out phone numbers as I desperately made notes on the scratch pad next to my keyboard on how the show might end. I tried a million ideas and none of them seemed to work. Andy was calling me weekly – just checking in to see how it was going. I assured him things were going fine – it was just taking slightly longer than anticipated. I needed a little more time.

It was during one of these calls that Andy brought up a slight problem the theatre was having with the show. The problem was the title. The title? Don't harass me about the title. I haven't even got a fucking third act. Of course I didn't say this. This was my professional debut. I didn't want to screw it up. Andy and various other people at the theatre (at this point it hadn't even really occurred to me that there were other people at the theatre I might have to deal with) felt that *Die Lycanthrope* was too hard to understand and people wouldn't know what they were coming to see. Could I think of a new title? No. I couldn't even think of an ending. Andy suggested *Wolfboy*. I didn't find it all that appealing but I had weightier things to consider and said sure. *Wolfboy* it was and *Wolfboy* it remained.

I was about halfway through the third act when I received another phone call from Andy. By this point I had come to dread Andy's phone calls. The theatre was worried. The clock was ticking and, because it was a brand new play by a brand new writer, they thought it might be wise for me to go to Toronto and work with the director who would be workshopping the script with some actors before we started rehearsals in Saskatchewan. Director? What director? No one told me there'd be a director. I thought I'd be the director. I'd always directed my own work before. Andy assured me that Layne Coleman, the director he'd chosen, was perfect for the project and would help me come up with that elusive ending. Again, to avoid rocking the boat, I acquiesced, quit my job (no trauma there) and got on my first plane for my very first trip to Toronto. It was September. I had started the play in July.

Layne Coleman, and his then girlfriend, Karen Woolridge (who would play Annie in the show), picked me up at the airport and drove me into Toronto. I was extremely hungover from a farewell party the night before and as we drove by the vast expanse of water next to the freeway in from the airport I asked if that was the Atlantic Ocean. Karen and Layne shared a quick look and notified me it was Lake Ontario. Must've been the hangover. I was driven directly to Theatre Passe Muraille to meet the actors and to hear the existing script read. I found it a little odd that no one had consulted me about the hiring of actors – but hey – I was new at this. What did I know? I listened to the reading through a pounding headache. I think that first reading – minus the last few scenes of the play which still weren't written – lasted three hours. Response from the actors was enthusiastic but we all knew it would have to be cut drastically. We also knew it needed an ending *now*.

I was driven from the theatre to the Waldorf Astoria Hotel on Charles Street. The hotel's gone now but at that time it was known as a theatrical hotel (meaning cheap) and a place where the government housed illegal immigrants until they could be deported. It was here that I saw my first cockroach, which fell on my chest as I lay in bed reading. It was also here that I saw my first centipede, which was six inches long and red, as it crawled from a crack in the wall around the shower-head while I bathed. It was also here that I holed up for three days drinking grapefruit juice and eating crackers while I wrote the end of the play. Layne, in the meantime, was rehearsing with Angelo Rizacos and Stuart Clow, who had been engaged to play David and Bernie, the leads. I'd usually knock off around ten in the evening and head into the gay village where I found my first taste of big city night life, pre-AIDS. It was exhausting, frightening and exhilarating.

Ultimately I came up with an ending I found satisfying. There was a sexual experience between David and Bernie, Bernie was unable to deal with it, the wolf power was proven to be a lie, and Bernie left with his father. David was left alone, haunted by Annie's ghost. Layne picked the script up and took it to the theatre for the actors to read. I was left in the hotel room to start making the cuts needed to get the show down to a manageable running time. Layne returned a short time later to say the ending wouldn't work. It wasn't dramatic and he and the actors had a major problem with the "fucking and sucking" aspects. Of course they did. He was straight. So were the actors.

We were just a few days away from flying to Saskatoon to start rehearsals. Layne and I spent the next three hours in the hotel room discussing the ending. Layne suggested a fight between the boys culminating in one of them getting stabbed. I took this further and suggested David sacrifice himself, allowing Bernie to return to the world, where he obviously belonged, by throwing himself on the knife while Bernie held it. Layne liked the idea. We both knew it owed a lot to *The Zoo Story*, but considering the play already owed a major debt to *Equus*, Jim Carol's *Basketball Diaries*, and the music of Bruce Springsteen and Graham Parker, I had no problem going with it. Besides, I was physically and creatively exhausted. I wrote the new ending, much of it according to Layne's specifications. Truthfully, at that time I saw no problem with what I now realize was his homophobic reaction to the ending. My own sexuality and the sexuality of my characters was something I was only just beginning to deal with and a public statement of the kind the original ending held was too much for me to handle in my early twenties. It would be a number of years before I started to deal with my own homophobia.

We flew to Saskatoon a short time later. Initially I sat in on rehearsals, but we all found it so difficult having an emotional and insecure playwright present that I was eventually asked to leave and was only too happy to comply. I hated watching these rehearsals. While both actors playing the boys were fine actors, I believed that they were radically miscast. I also thought Layne didn't really understand the world of the play. I still think this. Every once in a while I'd pop by to okay cuts which were still being made despite – or because of – my absence. I started writing another play in the orange shag-carpeted flat I was sharing with my friend Kat Mullaly, who had been brought in from Edmonton to play Cherry, the nurse. I read comic books. I walked the streets. I gave interviews and caused something of a sensation with my black and red leather jacket, spiky hair, and arrogant, outspoken attitude.

Two days before opening I dropped into the theatre to watch a technical run of the play. As the lights went down and Layne moved onto the stage to start his notes, I left the theatre, wandered into a pizza place, ordered a beer, and started to cry. Nothing in the play seemed to work. Everyone involved with the show seemed to hate the script and I felt like my career was over before it had started. If one's introduction to the theatre could be compared to losing one's virginity, I felt like I'd just been gang-banged.

The show opened a few days later and it wasn't brilliant and it wasn't horrible. It was something in between. The reviews were mixed, as was the audience response. Hardly the sensation I'd hoped for. I returned to Edmonton immediately. I wish I could say I'd learned a number of hard lessons that would make my life as a writer richer and easier. This wasn't the case. All I'd managed to do was survive. But, looking back at the experience now – the mad timetable, the length of the show, my age and inexperience – I now realize survival itself was something of a miracle.

The show went on to do something few other new Canadian plays enjoyed at the time. It was produced three more times. There was an Edmonton production at Theatre Network that, while better cast, suffered from soft direction. I rewrote the play for this production and berated the poor director constantly because he wasn't doing it *my* way. Reviews were positive. Box office was indifferent. There was a Vancouver production that the cast and director seem to have twirled together from various drafts of the script. It was a hit mostly because of John Cooper's direction and John Moffatt's performance. (John would go on to create the role of David in the original production of *Unidentified Human Remains and the True Nature of Love*.) And finally there was the Toronto production.

By 1984, when the Toronto show was produced, I must have rewritten the script 15 times. I rewrote according to directors' suggestions. I rewrote according to actors' suggestions. I rewrote according to dramaturgical suggestions. I rewrote according to critics' suggestions. I no longer knew what the show was about or why I originally had wanted to write it. I refused to rewrite anything for the Toronto production and I had no interest in attending rehearsals. The show starred Carl Marrotte (a fine actor who went on to television semi-fame in *He Shoots, He Scores*) and the then unknown Keanu Reeves. My opinion then was that Keanu wasn't a particularly good actor. Having watched his film career take off I can't honestly say that my opinion's changed. The show was a disaster. A confused script, the monstrous two-storey, raked set that defied all staging possibilities and John Palmer's direction, which veered from desperate to nonexistent, led to the worst reviews and audience reaction I have ever experienced in my life.

The failure of the show, a break up with a neurotic, abusive lover, and the impending AIDS crisis that was hanging over the Toronto gay community like a dark, heavy cloud, were the final straw. After three years in Toronto I left the city and the theatre – for good. Or so I thought.

Two years later I wrote *Unidentified Human Remains and the True Nature of Love*. When I sat down to write the play I promised myself I would take all the time I wanted and I would write whatever I felt like. I wouldn't censor myself and I wouldn't let anyone see it until I was sure it was finished to my satisfaction. And when it was finished to my satisfaction, I would not approve any directing, casting, or design decisions unless I was completely confident in them. *Remains* had its own traumas but, for the most part, I stuck to my guns, and the play has been what I intended it to be.

Remains wouldn't have been the hit it became without *Wolfboy* first. *Wolfboy* was a show that started out with great potential and gradually dissipated into confusion. No one, not myself or the directors or the actors or the theatres, can be blamed for what happened. The script's journey was arrested, by, if anything, too much enthusiasm. We all liked it too much and pushed it to production before it was ready. I thought I was brilliant when I was really only precocious. I struck an arrogant attitude and blamed others for my own shortcomings to make up for the fear and uncertainty I felt in a situation I wasn't quite ready for. But I don't regret a single moment of the entire experience. If nothing else, at least I was able to forgo some of the endless developmental hell my peers were subjected to (and sometimes still are). I made my mistakes and learned in the only real way a playwright can learn: on-stage, with a fully mounted show presented to a paying audience.

In preparing this play for publication, I have edited it extensively, done away with the difficult three act structure, cut one of the characters (Dr. Sherrot about whom I was always unsure), and changed the ending to what feels to me like a true conclusion to the show. It's embarrassing and hilarious, and sometimes a little sad, to look back at one's early work. Were I to write *Wolfboy* now, I'm sure I would write a much different play. But the play was a product of its times and has many strengths to recommend it.

Although the show is dedicated to my spiritual brother and best friend BJ Radomski, I must also dedicate it to Paul Thompson, Andy Tahn, and the directors, actors, designers, and technicians who survived it with me.

Brad Fraser
Toronto
May 3, 1993

First Performance

Wolfboy was originally presented at 25th Street Theatre in Saskatoon, Saskatchewan, directed by Layne Coleman.

Cast:

David – *Angelo Rizacos*
Bernie – *Stuart Clow*
Cherry – *Kat Mullaly*
McMillan – *Victor Sutton*
Annie – *Karen Woolridge*
Dr. Sherrot – *Jo Ann McIntyre*

Characters:

David Sawchuck
Bernie McMillan
Cherry Clipton
Walter McMillan
Annie Meyer

Setting:

The play is set in a boy's home/hospital. We see David and Bernie's rooms. They are separated by a door and each has a door leading to an outside corridor. We see the corridor.

Blackness.

A sudden spot on Annie.

Annie: David?

David rises from the bed in his room, dimly lit. He growls.

A light on Bernie in his room.

Bernie: It wasn't hard. Not really. I did it in a sink full of hot water. I read somewhere it didn't hurt as much if you did it in hot water. And it didn't. Not much. Everything just got red. Red. Red and black.

In his room, David moves to the door separating his room from Bernie's. He senses Bernie's presence on the other side. David growls quietly.

Lights on the corridor. Cherry and McMillan are there.

Cherry: Those cuts should heal in no time.

McMillan: Thank Christ.

Cherry: Shouldn't even leave much of a scar.

McMillan: Good.

Through this David has slowly circled toward the door leading to Bernie's room. A growl is building in his throat. Cherry leads McMillan out of the office and down the corridor.

Cherry: Look, you've had a rough night and it's a long ride home. Why don't you go get some sleep? Dr. Sherrot'll call you in the morning.

McMillan: Isn't there anything I can do?

Cherry: Not right now.

Cherry leads McMillan off. David, who crouches a foot from the door to Bernie's room, suddenly leaps at the door, clawing at it, and growling angrily. Bernie stares at the door. Cherry rushes back on. Bernie moves to the door and leans against it, hoping to hear what's happening on the other side. Cherry enters David's room.

Cherry: David?

David turns on her, snarling.

Cherry: What's wrong?

David advances on her.

Cherry: Stay back.

David continues to advance. Cherry backs away.

Cherry: I'll call an orderly.

David leaps at Cherry. She jumps out the door, closing it quickly, and locking it. David turns back to the door separating his room from Bernie's. He moves to the door and leans against it, mirroring Bernie's image on the other side. After a moment they both move from the door to their beds, mirroring one another again. They stretch out on their beds as the lights crossfade to the corridor. It is morning. Cherry is walking down the hallway, whistling to herself. She stops at the door leading to Bernie's room knocks and unlocks the door, entering. Bernie sits up.

Cherry: And how are we this morning?

Bernie: Fifty fifty. I'm fine but you look like shit.

Cherry: Time to see Dr. Sherrot.

Bernie: Piss off. *Short Pause.* Who's Dr. Sherrot?

Cherry: Runs the dump.

Bernie: Fuck her.

Cherry: Not her type.

Bernie: Fuck you.

Cherry: Nothing to be scared of.

Bernie: I'm not scared.

Cherry: That's not what those bandages on your wrists say.

Pause.

Bernie: How come you're so fucking fat?

Cherry: My mother loved me too much. Shall we?

Bernie: No.

Cherry: I can call an orderly.

Bernie: Those big goons wandering the hallways?

Cherry: They're very gentle.

There is a sudden, maniacal explosion of laughter from a nearby room.

Bernie: Jesus! What was that?

Cherry: Wally Simco. 13B.

Bernie: What's he here for?

Cherry: Raping his sister.

Bernie: Fuck.

Cherry: Shall we?

Bernie: I'm not telling her shit.

Bernie follows Cherry out of the room. Lights rise on McMillan.

McMillan: No. Don't understand it. Not a bit. Always been a good boy. Stable. Responsible. Great grades. Captain of the football team. Hockey. You name it. He's a good boy. Always was.

Lights rise on David's room. He is restrained in his bed with thick elastic straps. All the beds, including Bernie's, are equipped with such straps. There is a rubber ball appliance strapped into his mouth. The ball has a small hole in it for air. Cherry enters the room carrying a tray of food. The light remains on McMillan.

Cherry: Morning handsome.

McMillan: A plumber.

Cherry: Brekky.

McMillan: Okay, money.

Cherry: Hungry?

McMillan: Divorce. Right.

Cherry: Sure you are.

McMillan: Not such a big deal for a smart kid.

Cherry: That muzzle's a horror show huh?

McMillan: Didn't really know how to discuss it with a kid.

Cherry: Can't have you chewing on the staff though. Very anti-social.

McMillan: What's to discuss. She left. That's it. Nothing to be gained talking about it.

Cherry removes David's muzzle.

Cherry: And let's have an extra special thank you to the Marquis de Sade for his contribution to modern medicine. Now open wide and I'll give you some lunch. *David growls at her.* C'mon. *David refuses to open his mouth. She pinches his nose closed and pops a spoonful of food into his mouth when he opens it to breathe.* Gotcha! *David spits the food on her.* David! *Cherry rises with the tray.* Even Florence Nightingale wouldn't put up with this shit! *Cherry sets the tray down and puts the appliance back in David's mouth. She picks the tray up and exits.* Howl when you get hungry.

McMillan: Friends. I guess. There were guys he hung out with.

A light rises on Bernie.

Bernie: Dad's razor was so sharp.

McMillan: Girls. Oh sure. Pretty girls. Lotsa them.

Bernie: The skin opened up easy.

McMillan: Hanging around. Calling him.

Bernie: Like a zipper.

McMillan: Girls. Yeah.

Bernie: When I woke up he was holding me in the
ambulance.

McMillan: Sometimes he cried.

Bernie: His arms around my shoulders.

McMillan: In his room. At night.

Bernie: Red.

McMillan: Didn't know what to say.

Bernie: And black.

McMillan: Maybe I wasn't hearing right.

Bernie: No pain.

McMillan: He's always been the best kid.

Bernie: No gain.

McMillan: I don't know what else to say.

Bernie: Gone.

McMillan: Sure. I'll see him.

Bernie: Good bye.

David, strapped to his bed, the appliance in his mouth, wakes as Annie appears.

Annie: Hi. What's your name? Mine's Annie. What's your name? Mine's Annie. Mine's.... There's rafters.

As Annie speaks David madly struggles against his bonds. Lights crossfade to Bernie's room. Bernie is sitting on his bed. Cherry knocks, unlocks the door, and enters with McMillan.

Cherry: Your dad.

Cherry exits, closing the door after her. Bernie doesn't look at McMillan.

McMillan: Chuck called to see why you weren't at school this morning. I told him you weren't feeling well. Room's kinda small huh? Can't smoke anywhere in this fucking building. How're your wrists? They hurt?

Bernie: The skin opened up easy.

McMillan: Son?

Bernie: Like a zipper.

McMillan: They wanna keep you here for a while.

Observation. Whatever the hell that is. Just a coupla days. Whadaya think?

Bernie: Blood.

McMillan: Bern?

Bernie: No pain.

McMillan: I'll talk to you tomorrow.

McMillan exits. Bernie rolls onto his side on the bed.

Bernie: No pain.

Annie appears to David again.

Annie: I see you here. I see you here all the time. What's your name? Mine's Annie. What's your name? Mine's Annie.

Annie fades as David struggles against his bonds. Bernie hears him and moves to the door separating their rooms. Bernie tries the knob. It is locked. David whimpers. Bernie leans into the door to hear better. A light rises on McMillan.

McMillan: Little fingers. Little toes. Smooth skin. That baby smell. The way their heads wobble and they smile with no teeth. He was fucking perfect.

Bernie's room. Morning. Bernie lies on his bed. Cherry knocks, unlocks the door, and enters.

Cherry: You're up.

Bernie: Dr. Sherrot time.

Cherry: I can tell you don't like her.

Bernie: This place is boring.

Cherry: Only when you're confined to your room. The dayroom and the gym are quite entertaining. You should co-operate a bit and see them.

Bernie: When do I get outa here?

Cherry: I don't really know how that stuff works. I think they draw straws once a month. Kidding. It's got something to do with a deal between the doctors and your parents or something. I know if you want help they'll try to help you.

Bernie: They don't know me.

Cherry: Try talking to them.

Bernie: C'mon. They don't understand.

Cherry: They might.

Bernie: If I tell them about the abortion.

Cherry: Abortion?

Bernie: Liza.

Cherry: Liza?

Bernie: She was like my girlfriend.

Cherry: Like your girlfriend?

Bernie: Well we fucked a lot. So I guess that made her like my girlfriend. Liza was a real party girl. I think I loved her.

Cherry: Yeah.

Bernie: But then she got pregnant. That's heavy shit, man. We didn't know what to do. Like our parents ever talk about sex right. So she tried to do it herself. With a wire coat hanger. I found her in the bathroom. There was blood everywhere. I rushed her to the hospital. Our parents found out about everything.

Cherry: And was that why you tried suicide this time – or the last time.

Pause.

Bernie: How the fuck did you know about that?

Cherry: I work here.

Bernie: As a what?

Cherry: I help out.

Bernie: You're a fucking spy.

Cherry: The abortion story's real lame, Bernie.

Pause.

Bernie: I hear things. At night. In that room.

Cherry: David.

Bernie: Who's David?

Cherry: The guy they keep in there.

Bernie: What's wrong with him?

Cherry: Lycanthropy.

Bernie: Lycanthropy?

Cherry: Thinks he's a wolf.

Bernie: Shit.

Cherry: Come on.

Bernie: And I thought I was fucked up.

Bernie and Cherry exit the room as the lights rise on David's room. Annie appears to David.

Annie: You come here too much. All the time. It's cold sometimes. It's dark sometimes. Wanna see what my Uncle Bill taught me? I'll show you if you're nice. What's your name?

Lights rise on Bernie and Cherry in the corridor. Bernie carries a pen and a pad of paper.

Bernie: Write about my feelings. That's original. I'm gonna write about my zits. I'm gonna write about my fucking dick.

Cherry: That'll be a short piece.

Bernie: You're really fucking funny.

Cherry unlocks Bernie's door and opens it. She gestures inside.

Cherry: Write about your dreams.

Bernie: Maybe I'll use this felt-tip pen to poke through my eyes to my brain and kill myself.

Cherry: Start now and you'll be dead by Friday. If you break the plastic clip off you might be able to saw through your throat by Thursday.

Bernie: You don't act very professional.

Cherry: Neither do you. 'night.

Cherry closes the door and exits. Bernie throws the pad on the table and toys with the pen. In the next room, David whines. Bernie hears the sound. He examines the pen again then he breaks off the plastic pocket clip. He moves to the door to David's room and inserts the broken plastic clip into the lock. Bernie jiggles the clip around and rattles the door knob. After a moment the door clicks open. Bernie pulls the clip from the lock and regards the door in awe.

Bernie: Goddamn.

Bernie pushes the door open completely and steps into David's room. He sees David strapped to his bed.

Bernie: Jesus Christ. What the fuck have they done to you? Looks uncomfortable as hell. *Bernie moves to undo the strap across David's chest.* Let me – *David growls at Bernie viciously. Bernie pulls his hand away from the strap.* Okay. Okay. Stay tied up. Man you must be some kinda animal for them to have to do this to you. What're you in for? Pissing on fire hydrants? Hey, what's that little hole thing in your mouth thing for? Is that what you breathe through. I bet it is. What happens if I put my finger over it like this *does so* and pinch your nose shut like this? *Does so.* Bet it gets real hard to breathe. *David struggles madly. After a moment Bernie pulls away, letting David breathe.* Relax dogboy. I was only farting around. Just popped over to see what the creature in the locked room looked like. You're not so scary. Well except your hair. That's real scary. What'd you cut it with? A spoon? You talk? *Bernie removes the appliance.* Okay talk. Talk to me. Talk. What's your name? *David growls at Bernie.* If that's the best you can do I'd hold off going to Grandma's house for a while. *Bernie sits on the bed next to David.* What big teeth you have Grandma. Can't wait for the woodsman to get here Grandma – *David twists in his restraints suddenly and nearly bites Bernie. Bernie jumps off the bed.* Are you fucking nuts?! I'm telling you Rover, if you're not a good boy Daddy's gonna get very very mad. No. You're not a Rover. You're something smaller. Not Rover – Toto. You're a fucking Toto, man. You're a big disappointment, Toto. I'd work on that if I were you. Looks like I might be here for a while and I need something to keep me amused. After all, with you all tied up like this I could do anything I wanted to. Couldn't I?

Bernie slips the appliance back onto David and exits to his room, closing the door behind him. Annie appears dimly.

Annie: Cold down here. Dark. Smells like ants.

The light on David and Annie fades as Bernie lies down on his bed. There is a knock at his door. Cherry unlocks the door and enters.

Cherry: Lights out.

Bernie: Right.

Cherry: Father just left.

Bernie: Yeah?

Cherry: He was in Sherrot's office for over an hour. I think they're worried because you haven't asked to get out of your room yet.

Bernie: So I can hang out with the psychos? Get real.

Cherry: You dislike everyone?

Bernie: Sure. But you mostly.

Pause.

Cherry: Lights out.

Bernie: Yeah.

Cherry exits, switching the light off as she goes. Bernie sits on his bed. Cherry unlocks the door to David's room and enters.

Cherry: Gotta turn the lights out.

Bernie stretches out on his bed to sleep.

Cherry: That thing makes me sick.

Cherry removes the appliance.

Cherry: I've got the morning shift. I'll make sure no one knows it was off. Get some sleep.

Cherry exits. A spot on McMillan.

McMillan: Then they're walking. Then they're reaching out for you. Then they're starting to say stuff. But Jesus they're cute.

Annie appears in David's room.

Annie: David?

McMillan: And you want to teach them but you don't know what you think.

Annie: I can see you.

McMillan: So you just hold them a lot.

Annie: David?

David: *Quietly.* Annie?

McMillan: And hope you can protect them.

David: *Screams.* Annie!

Lights out on McMillan and Annie. As David screams Bernie sits up in his bed. He moves to the door and opens it.

Bernie: You talked. I heard you. You talked.

David growls at Bernie.

Bernie: Cut the shit. You said Annie. Who's Annie. *David growls a warning.* Sister? Mom? Aunt? Some fish you were boning? Hey, where's your thing? *Bernie sees the appliance on the table.* Thought I put that on. *He grabs the appliance and dangles it in front of David.* Who's Annie? Be a good Toto or Daddy'll get angry. *Pause. David watches him.* Okay. *Bernie starts to put the appliance back on David. David snarls and bites Bernie's hand. Bernie yells in pain and pulls away.* Shit! You fucking animal! *Slaps David.* Don't bite. *Slaps David again.* It's rude to bite people. *Slap.* People get mad when you bite. *Slap.* People get pissed –

Bernie raises his hand to slap David again then stops suddenly.

Bernie: Fuck.

Bernie exits to his room quickly, closing the door behind him. He moves to the bed and lies on it in a fetal position.

Bernie: No pain.

The lights change. Cherry unlocks Bernie's room and enters with McMillan.

Cherry: Three days now.

McMillan: Jesus.

Cherry: Won't talk. Won't eat.

McMillan: Bernie, you gotta eat.

Cherry: Doctors all say it's voluntary.

McMillan: Bernie – can you hear me?

Cherry: All the biological responses are normal.

McMillan: Bernie it's Dad.

Cherry: He's not even rude to me anymore.

McMillan: I thought you people were supposed to help him.

Cherry: It's not something we can do if he won't let us.

McMillan moves to Bernie, sitting near him but not touching him.

McMillan: What can I do?

Cherry: It's up to him.

McMillan: Talk to me.

Pause.

Cherry: Let him sleep.

McMillan: Yes.

Cherry and McMillan exit to the corridor as they speak. The lights on Bernie fade.

Cherry: Careful driving back. Roads are icy.

McMillan: I know.

Cherry: Full moon tonight.

McMillan: Oh yeah?

Cherry: Should be spectacular. The sky's so clear out here.

Fade to black. The sound of a winter storm is heard. It builds to a nearly deafening crescendo then fades. David speaks in the darkness.

David: You're not in Kansas anymore, Dorothy.

Lights snap up. Later the same night. David is standing over Bernie's bed wearing a leather jacket. Bernie is strapped to the bed.

Bernie: *Waking.* What the fuck?!

David: You're a pretty sound sleeper fella. You should watch that. People can do all kindsa rude things to you when you're sleeping.

Bernie: Oh shit.

David: Good thing all the beds come with straps.

Bernie: How?...

David: I get very strong when the moon is full. Like the leather?

Bernie: What are you doing to do?

David: I asked you if you like the leather, Dorothy.

Bernie: Let me go.

David: The leather, Asshole.

Bernie: Yes. I like it.

David: Me too. It was gift. From someone I usta know.

Bernie: Hey, all that shit when you were tied up – I was just kidding around.

David: Sure. You don't think I took that shit serious do you?

Bernie: You're talking.

David: Most comprehensibly. Like it?

Bernie: I knew it.

David: That wolf act didn't fool you, did it?

Bernie: No.

David: Smart boy.

Bernie: What are you going to do with me?

David: Whatever I want to.

Bernie: Untie me.

David: Don't like being tied up?

Bernie: No.

David: I brought something for you.

Bernie: What?

David removes the appliance from a back pocket.

Bernie: Christ.

David: Thought you might like it.

Bernie: Don't. I can't stand to have anything in my
mouth.

David: What a shame. You can miss a lot with those
kinda hang-ups.

Bernie: I'm sorry.

David: Not yet.

Bernie: Please –

David puts the appliance on Bernie. Bernie struggles.

David: There we go. Jeez, you know, when you're tied up
like that I could do just about anything I wanted to.
Couldn't I? *David takes a cigarette out of his pocket
and lights it.* They keep all our personal effects just
down the hall. It's easy as hell to get in. If you know
what you're doing. I got my jacket. I got my belt.
David takes his belt off. Nice huh. Shiny. I love this
belt. Do you love this belt, Dorothy? Do you? *Bernie
nods yes.* Bet it wouldn't even leave a mark. Let's see –
what else – *David reaches into his jacket and pulls out
a switchblade.* My blade. Hid it in the lining. Those
assholes never find it. *Flicks the blade open.* Nice huh?
Pretends to notice the bandages on Bernie's wrists for

the first time. What's this? You didn't go and do something silly did you, Dorothy? By golly, I think you did. You cut yourself all wrong. You should never slice your wrists crossways like that. It's very messy and seldom ever fatal. If you want to do the job right you should cut from the wrist to the elbow, like this. *He demonstrates, pressing the blade into Bernie's arm.* Severs a lot more of the important arteries and is just about impossible to fix. Silly silly mistake, Dorothy. Unless, of course, you weren't trying to kill yourself at all. In that case you did just the right thing to get the stupid ass kinda attention someone like you needs. *Takes the appliance off Bernie.* Were you trying to do the job right, Dorothy? Where you?

Bernie: Yes.

David: What?

Bernie: Yes I was trying to do it.

David: Do what?

Bernie: Kill myself.

David: You sure?

Bernie: Yes.

David: You positive?

Bernie: Yes.

David puts the knife to Bernie's throat.

David: Then you won't mind if I do the job for you.

Bernie: Don't.

David: You want to die, you want to die.

Bernie: No.

David: It's all death.

Bernie: It's not the same.

David: The same as what?

Bernie: As if I did it myself.

David: What's the difference?

Bernie: I don't know.

David: Explain.

Bernie: I can't.

David undoes the straps.

David: Get up.

Bernie rises.

David: Could you kill someone else?

Bernie: I – I don't –

David: *Cutting in.* Answer the fucking question.

Angelo Rizacos as David, Stuart Clow as Bernie.

Bernie: Maybe.

David: Maybe?

Bernie: It would depend.

David: On what?

Bernie: The person. The situation.

David hands the knife to Bernie. David bares his chest.

David: You want to kill me?

Bernie: What the hell are you doing?

David: Do it.

Bernie: Why should I?

David: I tied you up. Threatened to kill you. Doesn't that make you want to kill me?

Bernie: Yes. No. Fuck off.

David: Do it.

Bernie: You're crazy.

David: Do it.

Bernie: No.

Bernie throws the knife down. David snatches it up quickly and grabs Bernie by his shirt, viciously threatening him with the knife.

David: Get on your knees.

Bernie: What?

David: Just fucking do it, Dorothy.

Bernie gets onto his knees. David pulls Bernie's head into his chest.

David: Smell.

Bernie: Let me go.

David: I said smell.

Bernie: What the fuck are you doing?

David: Just smell.

Bernie smells David.

David: What do you smell?

Bernie: Nothing.

David: Try again.

Bernie: What am I supposed to smell?

David: Just smell. What do you smell?

Bernie: Sweat. Soap. I don't...

David: *Cutting in.* What do you smell?

Bernie smells David again. Pause.

David: What?

Bernie: Something.

David: Name it.

Bernie: I can't.

David releases Bernie.

David: The moon. Wind. Trees.

Bernie: *Unconvinced.* No.

David: You smell it. It's on me. *Short pause.* It's on you
too. Some of it. I smelled it the minute they brought
you in here.

Bernie: You're nuts.

David: Why didn't you use the knife?

Bernie: I don't kill people.

David: Just yourself.

Bernie: Get outa here.

David: Only fuck-ups kill themselves. Remember that, Dorothy.

Bernie: I should call an orderly.

David: Go ahead.

Pause.

David: I know you. I know you very well.

Bernie: No.

David: I can smell it and so can you. If it wasn't there – if I couldn't smell it – I'd kill you for what you did. Remember that.

Bernie: Get out.

David: Yeah. It's late. The moon's full. Don't come into my room tonight. It could be dangerous.

David exits. The sound of the wind outside builds. There is the howl of a wolf. The lights on the rooms crossfade to a spot on Annie.

Annie: I saw him in the park that time. On a bench. Just sitting. His head was kinda down and I knew he was like me. I knew it.

Lights rise on Bernie's room. Bernie has his shirt off and is doing push-ups on the floor. David enters from his room.

David: Morning.

Bernie: What do you want?

David: You're not too friendly this morning, Dorothy.

Bernie: You threatened to kill me last night.

David: But I didn't, did I?

Bernie: What?

David: I didn't kill you, did I?

Bernie: No.

David: Then what's your problem?

Bernie: You tied me up. Put that thing in my mouth.

David: What you did to me.

Bernie: I don't like to be threatened.

David: Then you shouldn't do it yourself.

Pause.

David: Sherrot started trying to get you to talk yet?

Pause.

David: Don't tell her anything. She'll fuck with your
head, man.

Bernie: I don't tell her anything.

David: You've got to be careful. They watch you in here.
All the time. They wait until you're sad – or something
– then bang, they're in there like flies to shit.

Bernie: How do you know?

David: I've been here before.

Bernie: Really?

David: Twice.

Bernie: Shit. What for?

David: Shit. What about them other guys in here?

Bernie: Fucking losers.

David: You got it.

Pause.

David: What's your name?

Pause.

Bernie: Bernie.

David: David.

Pause. They don't shake hands.

Bernie: Hi.

David: Hi.

Bernie: That shit when you were tied up – I don't... *Trails off. Shrugs.*

David: Shit gets crazy.

Bernie: Yeah. I –

David: *Cutting him off.* There's someone coming.

Bernie: What?

David: Talk to you later.

David exits to his room and gets under the straps. There is a knock at Bernie's door. Cherry unlocks the door and enters. She wears a whistle around her neck and carries a volleyball. She blows on the whistle very loud.

Cherry: Alright! Everyone out of the pool!

Bernie: Oh Jesus.

Cherry: You actually look like you might be alive today.

Bernie: Don't you ever stop?

Cherry: Dr. Sherrot'll be pleased.

Bernie: Fuck Sherrot.

Cherry: How's your spike?

Bernie: You'll never know.

Cherry: C'mon. You're a jock. One game...

Bernie: *Cutting her off.* I am not a jock.

Cherry: Okay. You're an athlete. Excuse me. Come on. We'll whip the orderlies.

Bernie: No.

Cherry: You need the exercise. You're getting pale and saggy like my parents. Come on. *Pause.* Suit yourself.

Cherry exits. Bernie moves to David's door. He is about to knock when David speaks to him from the bed.

David: It's open.

Bernie pushes the door open but doesn't enter David's room.

Bernie: One question.

David expertly disengages himself from the straps and sits up.

David: Shoot.

Bernie: How did you know she was coming?

David: Smelled her.

Bernie: Right.

Bernie pushes the door closed. A light rises on McMillan.

McMillan: He was always a good kid. Really good kid. *Short pause.* Really good kid. Didn't seem natural.

Bernie opens the door to David's room again.

Bernie: Smelled her?

David: Heard her too.

Bernie: That's weird.

David: Saved my ass more'n once.

Bernie: I don't believe you.

David moves across the room to close the door.

David: Fine.

Bernie: Wait.

David: What?

Bernie: People can't do stuff like that.

David: Wolves can.

David closes the door. Pause. Bernie opens the door.

Bernie: Can you prove it?

David: Thought I just did.

Bernie: Coincidence.

David: Don't say that shit, man. You sound like them when you say that shit.

Bernie: Who?

David: Them.

Bernie: Oh. Them. *Doesn't get it.* Prove it.

David grabs Bernie's shirt and abruptly pulls Bernie to him. He breathes deeply into Bernie's chest.

Bernie: Hey.

David releases Bernie.

David: You're 17 years old. You had instant eggs and sausage for breakfast. There are no women living at your house and you haven't had sex since – *sniffs Bernie again* – ever.

Long pause.

Bernie: You're nuts.

David: *Moving toward Bernie.* I can get more if you want.

Bernie: *Backing away.* No no. That's okay.

David: Scared?

Bernie: You're not really a wolf.

David: How can I do that then?

Bernie: You – you've been listening to me talk to that crazy nurse when she's in here?

David: I thought you didn't talk to them.

Bernie: I don't.

Pause.

Bernie: How long you been in here?

David: Three months or so.

Bernie: Jeez.

David: It's not so bad. Whenever they start hassling me I make like I'm gonna rip someone's throat out and they leave me alone.

Bernie: What're you in for?

David: Bit this jogger.

Bernie: What?

David: I hate fucking joggers, man. *Short pause.* I kinda lose control sometimes.

Bernie: They put you in here for biting someone?

David: They put you in here for not thinking like them.

Bernie: I think you're right.

David: This strappin' me down's shit though. Not into it. Almost time to take a hike.

Bernie: Leave?

David: Sure. Sneak out at night. This place isn't that well
guarded.

Bernie: Long way back to the city.

David: I'll thumb or hotwire a car.

Bernie: You can do that?

David: I can do anything.

Bernie: Then why are you still here?

David: Crashin' for the winter. It's not such a bad place if
you've got it together. Food's okay. It's warm.

Bernie: Why not just go home?

David: Haven't got one.

Bernie: Oh.

Pause.

David: Yeah. Time to blow this shithole. When it
warms up a bit.

Bernie: You know all about this place huh?

David: Guess so.

Pause. David moves toward his room.

David: Rounds pretty quick.

Bernie: I'll see you.

David: Count on it.

A light rises on McMillan as David returns to his room.

McMillan: Words. Questions. Talk. Talk talk talk. Everything's our fault. I just do what I was told to do. I just act like I'm supposed to act. That's all I can do.

David smells someone approaching. He moves into the bed and under the straps just as Cherry knocks, unlocks the door, and enters.

Cherry: Hiya. Not jumping nurses today I hope.

Cherry undoes David's straps.

Cherry: You've been pretty good lately. Dr. Sherrot says we can try removing the restraints. Don't screw it up. I have to yell for an orderly and you're in straps for the rest of you life. Good. Good David. Now how 'bout saying something?

Pause.

Cherry: Lights out.

Cherry exits and moves to the corridor door to Bernie's room. She knocks then unlocks the door and enters.

Bernie: One of these days you're going to do that and I'm gonna be pulling my rod or something.

Cherry: I'm hoping. Lights out.

Bernie: That guy in the next room?

Cherry: Yeah?

Bernie: Why's he here?

Cherry: We're not allowed to discuss the other patients.

Bernie: Really thinks he's a wolf?

Cherry: Yeah.

Bernie: Does he talk?

Cherry: Not since he got here.

Bernie: How can you stand this place?

Cherry: I like to help people.

Bernie: My dad called?

Cherry: I don't know.

Pause.

Cherry: Good night, Bernie.

Bernie: 'night.

Cherry exits. Bernie lies on his bed. A light rises on Annie.

Annie: David. That's a nice name. You live around here?
Didn't David kill that giant in the story? With a stone,
right? A stone.

David wakes suddenly, shaking and scared. His leather jacket is beside the bed. He fishes a cigarette out of the pocket and lights it. David moves to the door to Bernie's room and opens it. Bernie is sleeping soundly. David stares at Bernie until he wakes.

Bernie: David?

David: Hey, Dorothy.

Bernie: Scared me. What time is it?

David: Just after four.

Bernie: Where do you get those cigarettes?

David: Janitor's closet down the hall. Keeps all kindsa shit in there. Want one?

Bernie: I don't smoke.

David: Well la-de-fucking-da.

There is a loud, desperate laugh offstage.

David: Fuckin' loon.

Bernie: How do we get outa here?

David: Run.

Bernie: They let people out.

David: I've never seen it.

Bernie: Escape's pretty risky.

David: You don't get free without some risk.

Bernie: I don't know how to hotwire a car.

David: Then run.

Bernie: I can't talk to them.

David: Why?

Bernie: They want to know... *Trails off.*

David: Why you tried to off yourself.

Bernie: Yeah. *Short pause.* You ever want to do that?

David: I'm into life, man.

Bernie: They wouldn't understand.

David: Maybe they'd help you.

Bernie: Think so?

David: Not for a minute. *Short pause.* There's always the other alternative.

Bernie: What?

David: Tap your heels together three times and say "There's no place like home. There's no place like home."

Bernie: Get out.

David: Try it.

Bernie: Don't be stupid.

David: Might work.

Bernie: No way!

David: You ever tried it before?

Bernie: No.

David: Then how can you discount it.

Bernie: I don't believe in magic.

David: Shame.

Bernie: What?

David: Magic can help you.

Bernie: There's no such thing as magic. Or vampires. Or werewolves.

David starts to exit.

David: Okay.

Bernie: Hey.

David: What's the use of talking to you when I don't exist?

Bernie: You exist.

David: I'm also a wolf.

Bernie: You're serious?

David: Yeah, Mr. Hockey Player. I'm serious.

Bernie: How come you don't grow fangs and fur and all that stuff then?

David: That's horseshit, man. When you're a wolf you're not some kinda monster. You're just – more than everyone else.

Bernie: Like you have powers?

David: Something like that.

Bernie: How did you know I play hockey?

David: I read it in a fucking newspaper. What do you weigh?

Bernie: 160. 170. Why?

David moves to the table beside the bed.

David: C'm'ere.

Bernie: What?

David gets into an arm-wrestling position.

David: Let's go.

Bernie: You're half my size.

David: Scared?

Pause. Bernie gets into position to arm-wrestle with David.

Bernie: You're gonna get wiped.

David: Do it asshole.

They arm-wrestle. Bernie strains to put David down.

David: Well?

David puts down Bernie's arm decisively.

David: One more?

Bernie nods. They arm-wrestle again. David instantly puts Bernie down.

Bernie: Fuck!

David: Magic.

Bernie: You're nuts.

David: "There's no place like home. There's no place like home."

Bernie: Get real.

David: Take a chance.

Bernie: No way.

David: Try.

Pause. Feeling stupid, Bernie closes his eyes and taps his heels together three times.

Bernie: "There's no place like home. There's no place like home."

Pause. Bernie opens his eyes.

Bernie: It's not magic.

David: Maybe you didn't believe enough.

Bernie: As if.

David: Or maybe you were wishing for the wrong thing.

Bernie: Think so?

David: It's the first step, Dorothy.

Bernie: First step to what?

David: Oz.

Bernie: Is that where we're going?

David: We'll see.

David exits Bernie's room. A light rises on McMillan.

McMillan: But when they get older. That's when you have to be careful. Things change then. Feelings are different. They learn secrets.

Lights rise on David's room. David and Bernie are there. David wears his leather jacket.

Bernie: How much'd the jacket cost?

David: It was a gift.

Pause.

Bernie: You really not have a family?

David: Not worth talking about.

Bernie: What happened?

David: Old man took off when I was a kid. Old lady wasn't much good to anyone. Drank too fuckin' much. Beat me. Took off when I was about 13. Don't think she even noticed.

Bernie: By yourself?

David: Me and a friend.

Bernie: What did you do?

David: Stuff.

Bernie: What kinda stuff?

David: Panhandling. Shoplifting. Whatever.

Bernie: You made enough to live like that?

David: I don't think you wanna pursue this, Dorothy.

Bernie: Sure I do.

David: We did some hustling.

Bernie: You mean... like... pool.

David: No I don't mean like fucking pool.

Pause.

Bernie: Oh.

David: Right.

Bernie: With women?

David: With whoever wanted to get fucked by a 15 year old.

Bernie: What was it like?

David: Like having someone swing on your joint at 20 bucks a shot. It paid the rent. Kept us eating. Alive. Some people didn't even want your cock. Just to talk or whatever. Sometimes you had to slap them around a bit. One guy made me save my farts in a plastic bag.

Bernie: That's sick.

David: Sick don't mean shit when you're starving.

Bernie: What happened to your friend?

David: Boots? He died.

Bernie: Funny name.

David: His real name was Bartholomew. Who the fuck wants to be called Bartholomew?

Bernie: What happened?

David: ODed. Junk. This old pervert who collected our dirty underwear turned him on. Some political guy. Wife. Kids. The whole bit. Money. Fuckin' cunt got kids hooked and kept them in this apartment he had. That way he could use them whenever he wanted to. Boots got sucked right in.

Bernie: You ever done it?

David: Coupla times.

Bernie: How was it?

David: Not worth dying for.

Bernie: Still miss him?

David: Only when I'm awake.

Pause. David moves to the window and looks out.

David: Soon as this snow's stopped I'm outa here.

Bernie moves behind David and lays his hand on his shoulder.

David: Why're you doing that?

Bernie: You're sad.

David: No.

David pulls away from Bernie. Pause.

Bernie: Shit, does it get cold in here at night.

David removes his jacket and gives it to Bernie.

David: Here.

Bernie: Sure?

David: I don't feel the cold.

Bernie puts the coat on.

Bernie: David?

David: Yeah?

Bernie: Who was Annie?

David: Annie?

Bernie: That's the name you called that night.

A light rises on Annie alone. Bernie doesn't see or hear her.

Annie: Davey?

David: This girl – I knew.

Bernie: Was she – like your girlfriend?

David: No.

Annie: Davey?

Bernie: Where is she?

Pause. David doesn't seem to hear Bernie.

Bernie: David?

David: What?

Bernie: You listening?

David: Am now.

Bernie: This wolf thing –

David: It doesn't matter to me if you buy it or not,
Dorothy.

Bernie: It's too weird.

David: *Shrugs.* Yep.

Bernie: I mean – are there more werewolves out there?

David: Y'gotta know one to become one.

Bernie: Where do you find them?

Bernie yawns.

David: I found mine in a movie theatre.

Bernie: What was playing?

David: *The Wolf Man.*

Bernie: Naturally.

David: Best movie ever made. If you like kinda boring black
and white thirties movies. Lon Chaney gets bit by Bela
Lugosi and turns into a werewolf. Me and Boots usta go

all the time. This theatre uptown usta play it on Friday nights at midnight. At first we didn't know what we were gonna see. Just wanted someplace warm to crash for a coupla hours. Once it started though – we got right into it. After that we'd go every chance we could. Maybe I'll show you –

Through this Bernie has gradually fallen asleep. David shakes Bernie with his foot.

David: Hey, man.

Bernie: *Walking.* Huh?

David: Crashed.

Bernie: Sorry.

David: Gotta stash the jacket.

Bernie: Right.

Bernie removes the jacket, gives it to David and rises to leave.

Bernie: You tired?

David: Don't need much sleep.

Bernie: 'night Toto.

David: 'night Dorothy.

Bernie exits. The light does a slower fade on David who stands holding the jacket and staring at the door to Bernie's room.

David: You gotta be careful. Y'gotta be so fucking
     careful.

A light rises on McMillan.

McMillan: Why can't we remember what it was like better?
     It seems so far away – like a dream or an old black and
     white movie you saw on the late show a long time ago.
     What did we think? What did we feel? How did adults
     look? What did we know?

*A light rises on Annie as the one on McMillan fades. Their
speeches nearly overlap.*

Annie: If you be nice to people they give you stuff and if you
     keep secrets they give you stuff and if you be quiet they
     give you stuff. They show you things.

*A light rises on Bernie's room. Day. Cherry knocks at the
door then pushes it open. She peers in.*

Cherry: Bernie?

*Bernie is not in the room. Cherry enters and checks out the
room. She notices a pile of papers and a pen on the side
table. She moves over to them for a better look. Bernie
enters from the corridor. He is wearing a bathing suit and
there is a towel wrapped around his neck.*

Bernie: Can I help you?

Cherry: You haven't written a word.

Bernie: Not in the mood.

Angelo Rizacos as David, Karen Woolridge as Annie.

Cherry: At least you're exercising.

Bernie: I like to swim.

There is a burst of lunatic laughter offstage.

Cherry: Wally's not doing so well.

Bernie: Happens if you rape your sister.

Cherry: He's sad.

Bernie: So's the sister.

Cherry: You told Dr. Sherrot you'd write about your feelings.

Bernie: I don't have any fucking feelings.

Cherry: Everyone has feelings.

Bernie: What did you want again?

Cherry: Don't you want to get out of here?

Bernie: I don't know.

Cherry: You could go home.

Bernie: This place isn't so bad. The food's okay. Bed's soft.

Cherry: You're getting cynical.

Bernie: You're getting annoying.

Cherry: Sounds like my parents.

Bernie: Mine too.

Cherry: Aren't you bored here?

Bernie: *Shrugs.* Sure.

Cherry: Nothing to do. No one to talk to. Any place'd be better –

Bernie: *Cutting in.* No. Some places are worse. Way worse.

Cherry: Like where?

Pause.

Cherry: Where?

Bernie: You and Sherrot got some good cop bad cop thing going I don't know about?

Cherry: Just trying to be friendly.

Bernie: Don't.

Cherry: *Indicates the pen and the paper.* Gonna use those?

Bernie: No.

Cherry takes the pen and paper and exits. As soon as she's gone David enters from his room. He carries a Penthouse *magazine.*

David: Thought she was never gonna leave.

Bernie: Whadaya got?

David: The janitor's jerk-off material. There was an article on astrology I wanted to read.

Bernie: Right.

Bernie changes out of his bathing suit into his jeans and tee shirt as they talk.

Bernie: He gonna miss it?

David: It's smut pal. No one ever admits to it.

Bernie: *Has changed.* Let's see.

They sit on the bed and look through the magazine together.

David: What's the story on your old man?

Bernie: He's a prick.

David: What happened to your mom?

Bernie: Left. No note. Nothing. A year later he got a letter from her lawyer asking for a divorce. That was the last we heard of her.

David: That's kinda shitty.

David lights a cigarette.

Bernie: Don't you worry about cancer?

David: Not too fucking much.

Bernie: It's unhealthy.

David: So's slashing your wrists.

Pause.

Bernie: Why do you do that?

David: What?

Bernie: Talk to me like I'm stupid.

David: Cuz sometimes you're stupid.

Bernie: Thanks.

David: I don't think you've seen much.

Bernie: I'm the same age you are.

David: I was never your age. You're fine – you just
haven't suffered.

Bernie: I've suffered.

David: How.

Bernie: Stuff's happened.

David: What stuff?

Bernie: Stuff.

David: You don't wanna talk about it.

Bernie: Right.

David: That's exactly what I mean.

Bernie: What?

David: Thinking you can get away with doing only what you want to.

Bernie: Huh?

David: Forget it.

They continue to leaf through the magazine.

Bernie: I've never seen anyone with tits that big.

David: I have. But never on anyone that attractive.

Bernie: *Penthouse's* great. They always show pink.

David: Ever had any?

Bernie: Some. You know.

David: Yeah. I know.

Pause. They leaf through the magazine.

David: Listen. This kills me. "Dear *Penthouse* Forum. I would like to share an experience I had with you and your readers. Fucking illiterate. It started with this girl. I will call her Babs. Babs is a senior in the college I attend. She's a gorgeous red-head with 32 inch hips and the biggest mammary muscles I have ever seen."

Bernie: Mammary muscles?

David: "I had been trying to meet Babs for months but could never get up the nerve to talk to her. Well try to image my shock and surprise when, one day while I was showering, there was a knock at the door. I opened it to find Babs standing there. She gave no explanation for her unexpected arrival. She simply pushed her way into the apartment, closing the door behind her, pulled the towel from around my waist and dropped to her knees before me. She stroked my nine-inch love pump to a granite like erection and popped it in her mouth –

Bernie: *Laughs.* The children! The children!

David: Goes on to talk about how him'n Babs did it in every room in the apartment about a hundred times in one night – Bab's screaming "Give it to me Daddy" the whole time. It ends with "shortly thereafter I came" and is signed "Pleased in Pittsburgh."

Bernie: Here's another one. Dear *Penthouse* Forum, "I would like to tell you about an unusual experience me and a buddy of mine had. I will call him Dick. I'm not queer but.... *Bernie trails off reading to himself.* Oh.

David: *Penthouse* Forum has something for everybody.

Bernie: It ends with "shortly thereafter I came" too.

David: They all end like that.

Bernie: That's strange.

David: You know this isn't real, right?

Bernie: What?

David: Take it from someone who knows, Dorothy, there aren't nearly as many nine-inch cocks and perfect 38 inch tits in the world as *Penthouse* Forum wants us to believe.

Bernie: Boy you talk funny sometimes.

David: People are so fucked up they can't even figure this shit out.

Bernie: You don't like people very much, do you?

David: People suck shit.

Bernie: You're a person.

David: I'm a wolf.

Bernie: You're a person too.

David: It's like this. People – they live in Kansas. But wolves – wolves live in Oz.

Bernie: I really started something with that Toto crack, didn't I?

David: Just tryin' to put it simply.

Bernie: I'm not stupid.

David: Prove it.

Bernie: I'm just as strong as you are.

David: Prove it.

Bernie: I can't change what you think.

David: I changed the way you thought of me, didn't I?

Bernie: I guess – yeah.

David: If I can do that to you why can't you do it to me?

Bernie: I'm not sure what I think of you.

David: Maybe you should decide.

Pause.

Bernie: I like you.

David: And well you should.

Bernie: I'm me. It's all I can be.

David: And what's you? Some loser who cuts his arms open and acts like a fuck-up most of the time?

Bernie: I suppose you're better?

David: I'm in control.

Bernie: So how do I get to Oz?

David: Follow the yellow brick road.

Bernie: What fucking yellow brick road?

David: Your yellow brick road.

Bernie: I don't have a yellow brick road.

David: Then make one.

Bernie: I suppose I have to be a werewolf to do that.

David: It helps.

Bernie: You're fucking me up, man.

David slaps Bernie.

Bernie: That hurt.

David: Open your fucking eyes.

Bernie: Get out.

David: Fine.

David exits to his own room, closing the door.

Bernie: Oz! Fuck Oz!

Bernie moves to the door and opens it. David is standing on the other side of the door. David slaps Bernie. Pause.

Bernie: People've always given me whatever I want.
Always.

David: It's not easy being beautiful.

Bernie: I had this cousin. Ronnie. When I was like four my
parents used to put me to bed with him. He was 18 –
maybe 19. He got me to suck his cock. All the time.
When I got older he used to fuck me. He made me
promise not to tell anyone.

David: When Boots died I wanted to die too. It was like being kicked in the nuts – real hard. I hated him. For giving in to them. For fucking up. I didn't even go to his funeral. His parents blamed me for the whole thing. I went to the theatre instead. Watched *The Wolf Man* one last time for Boots. I was sitting there – numb – hardly seeing or hearing anything and someone sat down next to me. That's when I realized I was crying. The credits were rolling and I was sitting there with tears all over my face. The person sitting next to me took my hand – held it tight. We got up and left the theatre. Holding hands. I was led to this filthy old boarding house and up a flight of dim stairs. We went into this gray room. I looked up. There was this black guy. With sunglasses on. He was looking at me. It was a full moon that night. I could see it through the window behind him. He reached out and took me in his arms and I cried into his leather. He slipped the collar of my shirt over and bit my neck – bit me hard – till I bled. I remember thinking "Why doesn't this hurt. This should hurt." I felt something moving into me. Something like power. Something like strength. I was seeing things different. He was moving against me and growling. Something exploded in my head and I knew then I'd be alright. I'd make it. Next thing I remember was dressing in the morning to leave. I looked at him laying in the bed watching me leave. He looked so fucking sad.

Bernie: I want to be special.

David: You are.

Bernie: Good night, Dorothy.

David: Good night, Toto.

Bernie and David look at one another for a moment, then Bernie turns and exits to his room, closing the door behind him. Lights crossfade to the corridor as the sound of the wind rises. Day. Cherry enters, moving down the corridor with an armload of blankets. McMillan steps into the corridor.

McMillan: How is he?

Cherry: A little better. Swimming.

McMillan: Swimming. Good.

Cherry: Does Dr. Sherrot know you're here?

McMillan: We're meeting. I'm doing a lot of overtime. I was supposed to be here half an hour ago. I took the wrong hallway.

Cherry: Do you want to see Bernie?

McMillan: Not right now. Thanks.

Cherry: Alright.

McMillan follows Cherry off. David opens the door to Bernie's room.

David: He's here.

Bernie: My dad?

David nods.

David: Sherrot's office.

Bernie: Right.

David: What do you think he's saying to her?

Bernie: Lies.

A light on McMillan alone.

McMillan: I love him. I don't know why he's having
these problems.

David: Bernie?

Bernie: Tired.

David: Sure.

David returns to his room.

McMillan: He's always been like other boys. There's
nothing different about him.

Bernie: Red. And black.

McMillan: So why?

*Annie appears in David's room. David senses her
immediately.*

Annie: Hi. Hi.

McMillan: What is it that makes him do something
like this?

Annie: I saw you.

McMillan: What makes his life so horrible?

Annie: What's your name?

David: Don't.

Annie: I'm Annie.

McMillan: What makes him different?

Annie: David?

David: Leave me alone!

Annie fades.

McMillan: I dreamed about him last night. About when he
was just a kid. We were camping and he got lost
somehow. I was running through the brush calling for
him. Then I saw him up ahead. Standing by this tree.
There was another little boy with him. They were
holding hands. The other little boy looked at me, and I
thought I knew who he was, but I couldn't remember.
Then there was blood. Does he talk to you? What does
he say to you?

David pushes open the door between the rooms.

David: He's gonna come here.

Bernie: Now?

David: Right away.

Stuart Clow as Bernie, Victor Sutton as McMillan.

Bernie: Shit.

David: Why are you afraid of him?

Bernie: I don't know.

David: He's just a guy.

Bernie: He's my dad.

David: He's gonna want you to come home.

Bernie: *Skeptical.* Right.

David: It's Kansas, Dorothy.

David exits to his room, shutting the door just as Cherry knocks on the door to Bernie's room. She opens the door and enters the room. McMillan follows her.

Cherry: Remember to sign the clipboard on your way out.

McMillan: Right. Thanks.

Cherry exits, closing the door. Pause. McMillan looks at Bernie. Bernie looks away.

McMillan: How are you?

Bernie: Fine. You?

McMillan: Good. You look good.

Bernie: Thanks.

McMillan: Gave us all a bit of a scare. This is hard. This is very hard. I don't know what to say. I don't know what this means. But whatever it is I think we can deal with it. I think we can try. Come home.

Pause.

McMillan: Come home.

Pause.

McMillan: Say something.

Pause. Bernie turns away from McMillan.

McMillan: Listen to me you little bastard – I don't know what kinda shit you're trying to pull here but you're not going to get away with it. I've been just about as patient as I'm gonna be. This silent treatment shit is getting on my nerves and I'm not gonna put up with it anymore.

McMillan grabs Bernie and roughly turns him around.

McMillan: You hear me?

Pause.

McMillan: You hear me?!

McMillan shakes Bernie. Bernie glares at McMillan. After a moment McMillan lets Bernie go.

McMillan: I'm still your father. I can sign you outa here whenever I want to.

Pause.

McMillan: Good night, Son.

Bernie: Good night, Father.

McMillan exits. Bernie sits on the bed. David enters from his room.

Bernie: Got a cigarette?

David: You sure?

Bernie: I'm fuckin' sure.

David gives Bernie a cigarette and lights it for him.

David: He's scared.

Bernie: Scared?

David: Of what he feels. Of the things he thinks. Everything.

Bernie: Everything?

David: He's deformed inside.

Bernie: He just wants what's best for me.

David: *Laughs.* You guys always buy that shit, man.

Bernie: He's my father.

David: He even buys it. But it's bullshit. He doesn't love you, Bernie. He doesn't love anything.

Bernie: Shut up.

David: Okay.

Pause.

Bernie: Snow's stopped.

David: Yeah.

Bernie: When're you leaving?

David: Soon.

Bernie: I want to come.

David: No.

Bernie: What?

David: You're not quick enough, Bernie.

Bernie: I am.

David: You'd be meat in a week.

Bernie: I would not.

David: You're too soft.

Bernie: Then make me a wolf.

Pause.

David: I don't know if it works that way.

Bernie: Wolves are strong.

David: Yes.

Bernie: Wolves are special.

David: Yes.

Bernie: Wolves don't fuck up.

David: No.

Bernie: I want to be one.

David: I'm not sure how it works.

Bernie: I want to go with you.

David: Fuck off with that shit!

Bernie: Take me.

David: I'm not gonna watch you die, man.

Bernie: I won't die.

David: Shit.

Bernie: I won't leave you, David. I promise.

David: Fuck.

Bernie: Please.

David: It's not like you think, Dorothy. It's scary –
shit. Nurse. Be cool.

David exits to his room quickly, closing the door behind him.

Cherry knocks at Bernie's door then unlocks it and enters.

Cherry: I hear congratulations are in order.

Bernie: What?

Cherry: Your father arranged for your release. You're going home in the morning.

Bernie: He can't do that.

Cherry: He can.

Bernie: Shit!

Cherry: Bernie, we're not doing anything for you here.

Bernie: You're keeping me away from him.

Cherry: Is there something you didn't tell us? Has he ever...

Bernie: *Cutting her off.* Been anything other than a typical, uptight, over competitive father? No.

Cherry: Then there's really nothing we can do. I'm sorry.

Bernie: Yeah. Right.

Cherry: If you'd cooperate...

Bernie: Get out.

Cherry: Bernie?

Bernie: You think you're fooling me with this concerned volunteer bullshit? You think I don't know you got the hots for me? I could be a fucking axe-killer and you'd still want me, wouldn't you? You're pathetic.

Cherry: You might be right about the crush. But you're wrong with the pathetic part. At least I'm honest about what I feel.

Bernie: You're a fucking woman. You're allowed to be honest.

Cherry: *Laughs.* You're too much.

Bernie: Don't you fucking laugh at me.

Cherry: Or what?

Pause.

Cherry: What'll you do?

Bernie: Get out.

Cherry: This attitude of yours – it's not gonna take you anywhere good.

Bernie: Thanks for the advice.

Cherry: I hope you remember it.

Cherry exits. Lights rise on David's room. Annie is there.

Annie: Why're you always by yourself?

David: Please.

Annie: Take me with you.

David: Leave me alone!

Bernie pushes open the door between the rooms. Annie disappears.

Bernie: What?

David: Nothing.

Bernie: You heard?

David: I heard.

Bernie: We've got to do it.

David: Tonight. When the moon comes out.

Bernie: Tonight.

A light rises on McMillan alone.

McMillan: It's for his own good. It's because I love him. The hospital's not helping him. Nothing's changed. He'll be happier at home. All that psychology shit confuses us both. All that talking. All that sharing. He should be at home. Where he belongs.

The lights rise on David's room. David and Bernie are there. David is wearing his leather jacket. Night.

David: Tell me why you tried to kill yourself.

Bernie: Because I wanted to die.

David: Man, you've been lying for so long you don't even know it anymore.

Bernie: It's what I was taught.

David: Tell me why you tried to kill yourself?

Bernie: Because I wanted to talk to someone. Because I was lonely.

David: What else?

Bernie: Because I'm stupid. Because I'm ugly.

David: You're not ugly.

Bernie: Who was Annie?

David: This girl.

Bernie: Trust me, David.

Annie appears in a spotlight..

Bernie: I trust you.

David: This girl.

Annie: David.

David: I met her in the park. After Boots died.

Annie: Hi.

David: In the park.

David and Annie are singled out by spots. They do not play this to one another.

Annie: How come you always look so sad?

David: Beat it.

Annie: My mom says people who look sad can't find God.

David: Aren't you kinda young to be out so late?

Annie: My mom works at night.

David: Does she know wh re you are?

Annie: I'm very mature for my age.

David: Piss off, kid.

Annie: No wonder you got no friends.

David: You've got a real smart mouth.

Annie: You're an asshole!

David: Don't cry.

Annie: I'm not.

David: I'm sorry.

Annie: Shut up.

David: She kept coming back.

Annie: David?

David: Her mother spent more time at church than she did with the kid. The shit she filled Annie's head with.

Annie: People who hang around the park are bad.

David: So much shit.

Annie: If they're not careful they do things to you.

David: All fucked up.

Annie: I'm s'posed to hate it when people do things to me.

David: She didn't have a chance.

Annie: They'll lift up your dress and touch you in places they shouldn't.

David: When you grow up...

Annie: They'll do the bad thing to you. Mom says I should never do the bad thing.

David: With someone you like. It'll be good.

Annie: It's sick.

David: Someone will hold you and kiss you and make you feel safe.

Annie: Safe?

David: Safe.

Annie: Good?

David: Loved.

Annie: My uncle loves me.

David: Uncle?

Annie: We have secrets.

David: It was late. The park was empty.

Annie: He showed me things.

David: We were cold.

Annie: Things move. Tickle.

David: She wouldn't leave.

Annie: Where do you go at night, David? Does someone make you feel safe?

David: She fucking knew.

Annie: Do people touch you?

David: The moon.

Annie: I want to touch you.

David: Go home.

Annie: Your skin feels so soft.

David: Now.

Annie: Smells nice.

David: Don't touch me.

Annie: My friend.

David: Please.

Annie: Do you love your friends?

David: Stop.

Annie: I know what you do. Those men. I followed you.

David: Annie.

Annie: They touch you.

David: Don't.

Annie: My mom says it's wrong. What men do.

David: Don't touch me!

Annie: Show me a secret.

David growls dangerously.

Annie: David?

David: The smell of her all around me. Her blood. Her juices.

Annie: David?

David: She runs.

Annie: Stop it!

David: Into the trees. I follow. My clothes fall away. The moon. Pounding in my head. Singing. Pine needles under my feet.

Annie: No!

David: I'm hard!

Annie: No!!

The lights on Annie snap out.

Bernie: Jesus.

David: She was 13 years old.

Bernie: Christ, David.

David removes his shirt.

Bernie: David?

David removes his belt and hands it to Bernie.

David: Use it.

Bernie: What?

David gets on all fours, baring his back to Bernie.

David: For Annie.

Bernie: No.

David: It'll make me free.

Bernie: No.

David: If you're my friend.

Bernie: No.

David: She fucking hung herself, man.

Bernie raises the belt.

David: Do it. Do it now!

Bernie brings the belt down on David's back with a loud smack. The lights all snap to black except for a spot on Annie. The sound of the whipping is heard under Annie's speech.

Annie: It's dark in the basement. There's spiders. He told me not to worry, there were no spiders, but I knew there were. I found the rope he usta tie me up with when we were playing. The walls were wet. Smelled like ants. I wasn't bleeding or anything. I have a secret. I put the stepladder by the washer. It went right up to the rafters. Right up to the rafters. I have a secret.

The lights on Annie snap out. A light rises on David and Bernie. Bernie drops the belt, breathing very hard.

Bernie: Why?

David: I had to pay.

Bernie: You fuck me up, man.

David: I hurt her.

Bernie: It's what we're taught.

David: You're my best friend.

Bernie: I don't understand anything anymore.

David: You made me free.

Pause.

David: No one ever said getting there would be easy.

Bernie slowly removes his shirt. David moves toward him.

David: Open yourself up. To the moon. Feel it. In your blood. Singing in your head. Open up, Bernie. Wide. Wide. *David is now in front of Bernie, touching his chest.* Feel it. Strength. Power. Knowledge. From me. To you. Flowing. Like blood. Like brothers. Like wolves.

David bites Bernie's neck.

David: Now.

Bernie: David?

David: Wolves.

Bernie: David?!

David: Together.

David has sunk to his knees before Bernie, leaving a long smear on blood down Bernie's naked torso. The lights fade to darkness as the long, lonely howl of a wolf is heard. A light rises on McMillan.

McMillan: I know what he wants to talk about. I know what he thinks it is. I usta wanna talk about it too. Sometimes. I don't know why. I just wanted to talk about it. But I didn't. I mean...how can you? You can't. Just can't.

The lights fade to black. The sound of the wind rises with a light on David and Bernie in David's room. Bernie is wiping the blood from his body with his tee shirt. His pants are open. David stands a few feet away, looking at Bernie. Bernie can't look at him.

David: Bernie?

Bernie: There's no fucking power.

David: What?

Bernie: You're a fucking psycho, man. I can't believe you got me to swallow that shit.

David: Don't.

Bernie: Did we do all this just so you could blow me?

David: No. That was everything the guy did to me. Exactly.

Bernie: You are nuts.

David: You've got to have it.

Bernie: I don't.

David: But it's not in me anymore! I can't hear – can't smell –

Bernie: *Cutting in.* That's because it never existed asshole.

David: Don't call me asshole.

Bernie: No. You're right. We should call me asshole. I'm the asshole. I'm the fucking asshole who fell for whatever this was. Wolf powers. Shit!

David: You're my friend.

Bernie: How can I be your fucking friend when everything you told me is a fucking lie?

David: It's not a lie.

Bernie: Then why aren't I a wolf, David?

Pause.

Bernie: Well?

David: I don't know. Annie's gone.

Bernie: Why are you really in here, David?

Pause.

Bernie: Who are you?

David: Everything I told you is true.

Bernie: You were gonna make me special. You were gonna make me different –

David: *Cutting in.* You didn't believe enough!

Bernie: Stop it with the magic shit.

David: You never really believed me. That's why it didn't work.

Bernie: Get real.

David: It's in you but you can't use it.

Bernie: What?

David: Because you don't believe. Because you don't deserve.

Bernie: You're fucked.

David: Give it back.

Bernie: What?

David: It's not yours. It's mine. Give it back.

Bernie: I don't fucking have it!

David: I know how to use it.

Bernie: You were lying.

David: It's mine.

David pulls the switchblade out of his pocket and snaps it open. Pause.

David: I want it back.

Bernie: Hey man –

David: It's mine.

Bernie: Just relax.

David: I thought you were my friend. I thought you knew.

Bernie: I am your friend. I do know.

David: But you're just like the rest of them.

Bernie: Take it easy.

David: You don't understand!

Bernie: Put the knife away.

David: You fooled me.

Bernie: I didn't. It just – it didn't work like I thought. That's all. It's okay. Really. We're supposed to go away. Remember? You and me. We'll take off.

David: There's no power.

Bernie: We don't need the power, man. We'll be okay. Together.

David: *With less resolve.* No.

Bernie: We're buds, remember. Dorothy and Toto. We're going to Oz.

David drops the switchblade slightly, so it is not as threatening to Bernie.

Bernie: I was... I dunno... crazy I guess. It just wasn't... what I expected. A guy gets fucked up y'know.

David lets the hand holding the knife drop to his side. He looks very sad.

Bernie: You don't need to pulla knife on me – I woulda come around after a bit. I'm your friend, David. Your friend.

David: Yes.

Bernie: You're gonna take me to see *The Wolf Man*.

David: Yes.

David moves toward Bernie slowly. Bernie opens his arms to David.

Bernie: Your friend.

David: Bernie.

Bernie: Just like Annie. Just like Boots.

Pause.

David: Yes.

Bernie takes David in his arms and holds him very close.

Bernie: I'm sorry David. I'm really really sorry.

David: You think I buy this shit?

Bernie: What?

David brings the knife up quickly and stabs it into Bernie's stomach. Bernie screams.

David: Think you're fucking fooling me?

David pushes the knife up, cutting Bernie's stomach open. Bernie begins to bleed profusely.

Bernie: No!

David: I see through you.

Bernie: Please –

David: I see right through you.

David pulls the knife out when the blade hits Bernie's sternum. Bernie holds his stomach, stumbling forward slightly. Blood spills from his stomach to the floor. He looks at the blood and at David with disbelief.

David: I'm not fucking stupid you know! You'd fuck off! You'd fuck off just like the rest of them!

Bernie: No –

David: The power's mine.

Bernie: I meant it.

David: And I want it back.

Bernie: Meant it.

Bernie falls to his knees.

David: The blood.

Bernie: Please – David – call someone – call...

David: I don't think so, Dorothy.

Bernie: *Screams out.* Help. Someone. Help me!

David moves behind Bernie putting a hand over his mouth to stop the screaming. Bernie struggles but is too weak to throw David off. David holds Bernie's head still.

David: Don't make it worse, Bernie. Just relax.

Bernie stops struggling, leaning back against David. David holds him tenderly.

David: Don't scream.

Bernie nods. David removes his hand from Bernie's mouth.

Bernie: Hurts.

David: Ssh.

Bernie: Please.

David: It's okay.

Bernie: I don't want to die.

David: You won't.

Bernie: Call someone.

David: My blood is in your blood. Your blood is in my blood.

Bernie: David?

David: My blood in your blood.

Bernie whimpers weakly. David reaches down with one hand and scoops a handful of blood from Bernie's wound.

David: My power in your blood.

David drinks the handful of blood, smearing his face with it.

David: My power in my blood.

Annie appears in a spot.

Annie: David?

David: Hi.

Annie: Why'd you send me away?

David: It's okay. I didn't mean it.

Annie: I don't like to be alone.

David: You won't be. Not anymore.

Annie: I love you, David.

Bernie looks at Annie. He can now see her.

Bernie: I'm cold.

Karen Woolridge as Annie.

Annie: Hi.

Bernie: Hurts.

Annie: It'll stop. You'll like it.

David takes another handful of blood.

David: Your blood in my blood.

Bernie: Meant it.

David drinks the blood.

David: You'll never die.

Bernie looks at David, his mouth working as if trying to speak. He raises a hand to David's face and touches it weakly. David smears his bloody face against Bernie's.

Bernie: *Weakly.* Cold.

David: You'll never die.

David pulls Bernie in tighter to him, cradling his body tenderly. Bernie's eyes close. He breathes with great effort. David speaks with great wonder.

David: You'll never ever die.

Slow fade to black.

PROM
NIGHT
OF THE
LIVING
DEAD

PROM NIGHT OF THE LIVING DEAD:

PLAYWRIGHT'S INTRODUCTION

The Citadel Theatre Teen Festival of the Arts was begun by
Wayne Fipke in 1988. It was a unique and important festival
in Canada. Unique because in its first four years, it
commissioned scripts from Canadian playwrights written
specifically for a teen audience and teen performers.
Important because by developing this adolescent audience,
the Citadel was doing the theatrically unheard of thing by
actually looking to the future in terms of audience and
professional development. It also provided Canadian writers
the rare chance to have their work performed on the Citadel
stages and opened those same stages to directors who might
not otherwise have had the opportunity to work in that
particular theatre. The festival was also creating a repertoire
of new plays written for teen audiences by some of the
country's most interesting writers, including Stewart
Lemoine, Michael D.C. McKinlay, Conni Massing, Kent
Staines, Jeffrey Hirschfield, and Robert Clinton.

I got involved with the festival in its second year,
directing Jeffrey Hirschfield's *Blood Buddies*. Fipke had
moved on to other things, and the festival was then run by
Gail Barrington Moss who was to leave the next year to be
replaced by Lindy Sisson. Under Sisson's direction the festival
would flower and begin to realize its true potential. In the
festival's third year I would rewrite an earlier script, *Young*

Art, and stage it in the Rice Theatre, at one time one of the Citadel's most interesting spaces.

When Lindy approached me about another show for the third year in a row, I was slightly reluctant. Although I loved the festival, I had some reservations. The commission money was a joke; the lead time for the writing of the plays was incredibly short; the week of open auditions, while usually exhilarating, could also be gruelling. The directors of the shows often saw up to 400 kids over five days. The three and a half months of afterschool and weekend rehearsal was a full time commitment that left little for anything else. But the biggest drawback was the sharing of stages.

In previous years two shows had to share each stage, making the one week technical time a nightmare and necessitating a set changeover between shows that severely limited the design capability for each play. I explained my reservations to Lindy. She agreed with me and had already addressed a number of these concerns. I told her if I was going to do the festival again, I wanted to do something I'd never be able to do anywhere else. I wanted to write a *big* musical for the 800 seat Shoctor stage. And I meant *big* – going so far as to consider a cast of up to 100 teens. Lindy was excited by the idea. I was contracted for the show and promised I would have the Shoctor Theatre and a full week of technical time all to myself.

I contacted the very talented Darrin Hagen, who had done a live score for *Young Art,* about writing the music. He was slightly hesitant as he'd never written a musical before. I assured him that I hadn't either, but the Teen Festival was a great opportunity to take chances and it would be a fabulous environment for us to learn in. Darrin accepted, and we started work on *Prom Night of the Living Dead.* We had exactly nine months before we opened. We knew the idea was madness but fuelled by an intense enthusiasm for the festival, the true joy of working together, and bags and bags of pot, we started. We did a quick outline of the show, the characters, the plot line, potential numbers etc. Then I'd write five or ten pages of book and lyrics and Darrin would immediately take them away and start setting lyrics to music. I finished my first draft in January, just in time to fly off to Chicago for the first American production of *Unidentified Human Remains and the True Nature of Love*, while Darrin finished the score. I returned a month later in time for a quick rewrite and edit, and we went immediately into auditions.

For a week we sat on the stage of the Maclab Theatre with the other playwrights and directors. Every day from ten until six we saw scores of young people swallow their fear and show us their talent. I'd come to realize the original idea of a cast of 100 would be impossible and had winnowed the number down to 50, 25 boys and 25 girls. In working with teens one learns quickly that there are always many more talented young women than young men. Consequently we had decided to turn most of the male characters into zombies as quickly as possible and to leave most of the hard stuff to the girls, with only a small number of principal roles for the guys. It's heartbreaking to sit through auditions and see so many talented and enthusiastic young people work desperately to have any part in a play. I was particularly touched by three of the teens we saw. One was a deaf boy who had auditioned for the festival in each of the previous years I had worked on it. This young man had lost his hearing gradually and was still learning to cope with the challenge. I admired his guts and his tenacity. Another one was a young black girl who had a crippled leg but sang like a young Jennifer Holiday in training. The last was a transfer student from Hong Kong whose command of English was tenuous and with absolutely no acting experience. But it was clear each of these kids wanted to be in a show and, since the play was essentially about being different, I decided I had to use them.

We cast the show – the number now increased to 53 – and started rehearsals. What followed was one of the most exciting, happy and challenging periods either Darrin or I have experienced. We had a real mixed bag of kids to deal with. Some were experienced and accomplished enough to be professionals. Others had never set foot on a stage before. Some were middle class, some came from disadvantaged backgrounds, some were black, white, oriental – we covered the spectrum. We, along with the choreographer Andrea Rabinovitch, designer Brock Lumsden, and our fabulous student stage management team, spent the next three months bringing this diverse group together in an ensemble that would ultimately become seamless. And it wasn't just stagecraft they were learning. We also explored all the underlying issues of the play, including society's treatment of women, homosexuality, and cultural differences. The kids were unbelievable in their discipline and eagerness. It was truly a life-altering experience for us all. The focus and commitment the cast demanded from Darrin and me was amazing – but what they gave us in return was worth every bit of energy we expended.

Two weeks before opening we moved into the Shoctor rehearsal hall in anticipation of our move onto the stage and our full week of tech. Then I was told the theatre had decided to hold over *The Mousetrap*, currently running on the Shoctor, and our tech week was cancelled.

I was stunned. I had been promised that week. I had 53 kids who needed to work on a stage that would contain four drops, three traps doors in the floor and five trucks (large, movable set pieces), not to mention the fact that 10 of them would be wearing body mikes. It was death for the technical end of the show and it was also dangerous to put that many inexperienced people on a stage when the design was as complex and mobile as ours. Through a series of unfortunate, accidental maneuvers by various festival organizers, I ended up in Robin Phillips's offices to explain why we had to find some sort of compromise. While I understood the Citadel's need to garner the revenue from this rare hit to offset its deficit, I also felt it was suicidal for me to open a show of this magnitude without any technical rehearsal. There had to be a reasonable way for us to get some stage time and still keep *The Mousetrap* open.

The conversation that ensued has become the stuff of Edmonton theatre legend. I don't see any point in recounting it now, except to say that I never said, as I have often been quoted as saying, "Do you know who I am?" to Phillips. I'd met with the man a number of times previously, and he knew full well who I was. Phillips suggested firing me. I told him he could go ahead, but if he did I had 53 kids who would leave with me and, since the show was already 80 percent booked, he might find that slightly detrimental to the festival's fiscal well being. He then launched into a tirade that, as far as I could tell, had absolutely nothing to do with the matter at hand. I left his office in mid-tirade, walked down to the rehearsal hall, told the cast exactly what happened, and we, as a group, walked out of the theatre.

The next morning the general manager of the Citadel was on the telephone wanting to know if there wasn't some way we could patch things up. We met, *sans* Mr. Phillips, a midnight strike of *The Mousetrap* was arranged, and our first performance was cancelled, giving us a total of two days on the stage to run our complicated technical rehearsal, less time than I had with *Blood Buddies* when I was sharing the stage with another show. Frankly, I wanted to cancel the show. But there were 53 kids and three and a half months of hard work, horrifying accidents, and moments of the most raw theatrical magic I've ever experienced that I couldn't turn my back on.

We opened the show. The first few days were rough. The script was still too long and the sound, through lack of time with the technology and the technicians' lack of knowledge of the show, was a nightmare. The reviews were scathing. But we made cuts to the show as it was running and the technical problems were finally ironed out. The cast was astounding, and it was the highest grossing Teen Festival show in the festival's history. It also received a standing ovation after every performance.

It had been a very lively nine months. Darrin and I came out of it feeling as if we had given birth. The show was picked up by two Albertan film producers shortly after it closed. Darrin and I took a much needed break from the material for a few months then started to rework it with an objectivity we hadn't had time for the first whirl around.

In the two years since then we have extensively reworked *Prom Night of the Living Dead* for the stage and the film – while working on another musical, *Outrageous*. We've cut the show mercilessly and focused it with a clarity the original lacked. We are now amazed at our ambition and our folly. We literally don't remember how we did it. Both of us have strong memories of being slumped over the piano, too stoned to sit erect, croaking out things that sounded like songs. I vaguely remember directing it. He sort of remembers scoring it. It seems like a million years ago, and the two men who wrote that show seem like other people now. It was an all consuming madness, and I can honestly say I have never had so much pure, unadulterated, undiluted, exhilarating *fun* in the theatre, before or since.

Unfortunately that Teen Festival no longer exists. The original script concept of plays by professional writers was deleted by Robin Phillips and those in charge of the Citadel. Aided in the argument for change by the local theatre press, Phillips and the Citadel decided that the new play element and high production values detracted from the work of the teens themselves. In a sense this was true. From the inception of the festival, the Edmonton theatre reviewers had refused to treat the event as anything other than a series of openings of new Canadian plays by interesting Canadian playwrights for the usual Canadian theatre-going audience. The people who made and supported this decision were not clued into the fact that what we were trying to do – every one of us who wrote for that festival – was to attract a new audience into the theatre by telling stories we hoped would appeal to them in a dramatic vocabulary they might understand. We weren't always successful, but all involved in the creative end of the Teen Festival did the best to make the theatre an exciting place for a young person to be – regardless of what side of the footlights they were on. Writers, directors, and designers were learning to work on productions far larger in size and scope than anything they'd been allowed to experience before. A repertoire of new plays was being developed for an audience that traditionally farts and giggles when placed in a theatre. And, most importantly, an entire generation of adolescents in one city learned to respect and welcome new work in the theatre. To those young people who became adults in the festival's first five years, a new play is no different that an existing play except perhaps in its sense of immediacy and timeliness. For them new Canadian work is not the exception. It's the norm. And the loss of that fostering of an audience and attitude is a loss of national proportions that we will all regret in the future.

But the loss isn't a total one. Those of us who wrote and directed for the festival worked with hundreds of teens. I've probably met a couple hundred myself. I remember most of their names and certain names keep popping up – some more and more insistently. All of them are on the fringes of Edmonton's very healthy theatre scene. Some are acting, some are working as stage managers, some are directing, and quite a few seem to be writing. A couple of them have mounted an alternative Teen Festival of sorts in nearby St. Albert where they première new works by teen writers. Others have produced independent shows around town. Many have now been through the University of Alberta acting program and are working their way into the profession. I lay no claim to the talent and ambition of these people. Like all of us, they got where they are on their own. But I like to think that, if there's one thing they learned from those of us who attempted to give their talent shape and a place to live, the one thing would be that theatre can exist anywhere, under any circumstances, provided the people creating it want it to happen more than anything else in the world. And I hope that when the day comes when I'm running a major regional theatre and I'm cancelling some inexperienced young director's technical time so I can hold over a mediocre, money-making show, he or she will have the nerve to take the cast and walk out of rehcarsal because every director should have the opportunity to prove they can.

Brad Fraser
Toronto
May 6, 1993

For Chad Cole, Kevin Hendricks, and the fifty-five young people who worked on the original production of the show.

First Performance

Prom Night of the Living Dead was premièred in the Shoctor Theatre during the Citadel Theatre's Edmonton Teen Festival of the Arts in May, 1991. It was directed by Brad Fraser with musical direction by Darrin Hagen, choreography by Andrea Rabinovitch, and design by Brock Lumsden.

Cast:

Lon – *Chad Cole*
Fern – *Bridget Ryan*
Dawn – *Leighana Shockey*
Butch – *Christopher Craddock*
Uncle Bill – *Cesar Suva*
Morgan – *Juliana Pivato*
Count Karma – *Clinton Carew*
Shape – *James Viveiros*
Tod – *Ross Smith*
Heidi – *Mindy Mathes*

THE GIRLS:

Stella – *Trina Davies*
Irene – *Monica Roberts*
Melody – *Christine Laurie*
Charlene – *Angelica D'Auteuil*
Debby – *Vera Macek*
Muffy – *Yolanda Kercher*
Buffy – *Danielle Mitchell*
Haley – *Karena Davis*
Nancy – *Elyne Quan*
Loretta – *Julie Shinyei*
Jenny – *Natalye Vivian*

THE JOCKS:

Goon – *Rick Harcourt*
Brent – *Ian Box*
Dick – *Laurence Miall*
Roger – *Kris Loranger*
Stu – *Dion Johnstone*

THE POOL HALL BOYS:

Huey – *Alan Miller*
Duey – *James Fraser*
Crick – *Jason Campbell*
Ben – *Kurt Spenrath*
Marty – *Diego Ibarra*
Arty – *Jung Luu*
Stan – *Jeremy Strautman*
Spaz – *Chris Dodd*
Liver – *Brian Leonard*
Muzzy – *Jeremy Johnson*

THE BRAINS:

Barney – *Chris Fassbender*
Ferd – *Conrad Chan*
Doody – *Rob Monk*
Ray – *Nathan Armson*
Bruce – *Krystof Lindenback*
She-wolf – *Neon*
Werewolf – *Tim Sell*

OTHER GIRLS:

Jenny Pahl, Amy Berger, Tina Stewart, Amber Pikula, Tanya Binette, Melody Carew, Sarah Ransaw

Dance Captain – *Lisa Meraw*

Characters:

Lon, a young man, 17
Fern, a young woman, 17
Dawn, a young woman, 17
Butch, a young man, 17
Tod, a young man, 16
Bill, Lon's Uncle, late 20s
Morgan, the new girl in town
Heidi, a ghost
Karma, a vampire
Shape, a frankenstein monster
She-wolf
Werewolf

THE GIRLS:	THE JOCKS:	THE HEADS:	THE BRAINS:
Stella	Brent	Muzzy	Barny
Irene	Goon	Duey	Ferd
Melody	Rod	Crick	Doody
Debby	Dick	Spaz	Bruce
Charlene	Liver	Ray	
Haley			
Muffy			

Various other kids from town. Roles can be doubled.

Setting:

The small city of Lester. Various locations.

Overture.

*An isolated spot. Uncle Bill stumbles onto the stage. The
entire scene is backlit and underscored. Bill is breathing
heavily and obviously hurt. He stumbles and clutches his
side in pain before running off the opposite side of the stage.*

*Spot on another area. Lon and Fern are walking hand in
hand.*

Fern: What are you thinking about?

Lon: The future.

Fern: Right.

Lon: Fern, we're nearly out of high school.

Fern: The prom's on Saturday night.

Lon: And after that, graduation.

Fern: Are you worried?

Lon: I don't know.

*Shape, Heidi, and Karma run into the spot where Bill was
seen. Like Bill, they are seen in silhouette. They stop and
look around desperately.*

Heidi: Which way?

Shape: There.

Karma: No. Here. I can smell his blood.

*The monsters rush off in the same direction as Bill. Lon and
Fern are see in their light.*

Brad Fraser and cast member Tina Stewart in rehearsal.

Lon: Fern?

Fern: Yeah?

Lon: Do you believe in fate?

Fern: You mean magic?

Lon: Sort of.

Fern: There's no such thing.

Lon: No?

Fern: Not in Lester.

Lon: I guess you're right.

Fern: Lon, I'd better get going. I'll be late.

Lon: I'll see you tomorrow.

Fern kisses her hand and playfully slaps it on Lon's face.

Fern: Count on it.

Fern exits. Morgan appears in the first spot. She is seen only in silhouette. She stops and looks around quickly.

Morgan: I can sense the power!

As the first spot dies Morgan exits in the same direction as the monsters . Lon and Fern are seen in separate spots.

COME ON FATE

Lon: Somewhere

Fern: Somehow

Dawn and Butch are picked up in separate spots.

Dawn and **Butch**:
              Someday *(repeat)*

Lon: I'll live somewhere

Fern: I'll live somehow *(overlapping)*

Tod is picked up in a separate spot.

Tod, Butch, and **Dawn:**

> I'll live someday

All five:

> Someplace I've never seen before
> Someplace I've never been before
> Someplace where people aren't the same
> And they all know my name
> Someplace where the wildlife's not so tame
> Someplace where everything's not so lame

Lights rise on the other characters as they join the song. The town of Lester is illuminated behind or around them.

All:

> Someday
> Somewhere
> Somehow
> I'll live
> But I want it now
> I want it now

Dawn:

> I can't wait

All:

> I want it now

Butch:

> I know I'll rate

All:

> I want it now

Fern:

> Before it's too late

All:

> Something's rising
> Something's pushing
> Something's growing
> Something's ripping
> I can't wait

For my fate
I WANT IT ALL NOW
Come on Fate, come on, come on
I can't wait, you're already late
Come on Fate, come on, come on
Feel my need, don't hesitate, c'mon

All the kids come together into a large group.

It's a new day, it's a new age
I have a new body, I have a new rage
Let me know now, let me know soon
Show me a picture, teach me a tune
Get me the hell out of this town
Take me to a place that's not so damn brown
Somewhere that's shiny with lots of new faces
Somewhere filled with adventure and exotic places
Somewhere where people know who they are
Somewhere that's greener, somewhere that's far
Somewhere that's far
Come on Fate, come on now
Come on Fate, come on now
Come on Fate, come on, come on
Come on Fate, come on, come on, come on,
    come on

The kids move away from one another, becoming isolated once again.

COME ON FATE *(personal version)*

Lon: *(Softly)* Come on Fate, come on, come on
Come here to Lester where I'm rotting away

Butch: Come here to Lester, come here today

Tod: Come here right now, before the sun starts to drop

Dawn: Come here right now, to the town hell forgot

Boys: Come for me

Girls: Come for me

Lon: Come here for Lon now, he's not such a jerk
                  He doesn't have it together, but he's doing the work

Fern: Someday he'll be the guy who knows who he is
                  Someday he'll crackle, he'll sparkle and fizz

Lon, Fern, Tod, Butch, and Dawn:
                  Someday we'll know why we're really here
                  Someday we'll know which direction to steer
                  To get clear out of here without fear

All: Come on Fate, come on, come on
                  Come on Fate, come on, come on, come on,
                     come on, come on

All characters begin to leave the stage as the chorus sings.

LESTER'S THEME

Chorus: Lester is a little town
                  In a little place
                  Surrounded by dust and cowshit
                  Cow shit, cow shit
                  It's surrounded by dust and cowshit

Lon is left alone on the stage. He is walking past a graveyard. The music becomes eerie. Lon nervously glances over his shoulder.

Lon: Later than I thought.

A shadowed figure steps from the gloom. Lon gasps and freezes. Bill stumbles into the light. One side of his face is badly wounded and he clutches his side in pain. Lon gasps.

Lon: Uncle Bill!

Bill: Hey Lon.

Lon: Jesus! You look terrible! Sit down.

Bill: I think I'd better.

Lon: What are you doing here? No one told me you were coming. I'll get Dad.

Bill: No!

Pause.

Lon: Someone beat you up or something?

Bill: You might say that.

Lon: I hope it wasn't those guys at the pool hall.

Bill: It wasn't anyone you know.

Lon: Then who?

Bill: Someone full of hate and spiders and puss
              Someone consumed with a hot, endless lust

Lon: Who?

Bill: A woman so evil her heart's polished steel
              A woman so frozen she doesn't know how to feel

Lon: Who is she?

Bill: Morgan

Lon: Morgan? Who's Morgan? Where have you been? We
          haven't heard from you in years. What's happening
          Uncle Bill?

Bill: I've been away Lon, far away Lon
              I've seen things Lon, I've been changed Lon
              My eyes have been opened to a world I never knew
              And the things that I've seen turn my blood into ice
              I've learned that the things I once thought were true
              Are just a veneer covering maggots and vice
              It's dark world, it's a dark world I've seen
              It's a strange place, a strange place I've been
              There are secrets untold that are centuries old
              There are monsters and terrors that wait to unfold
              It's a dark world. It's a dark world I've seen
              There are things out there Lon, we can't begin to
                 expect
              Things that feed on us humans without due respect
              They watch us, they stalk us, we have what they need
              They smile when we're hurt and laugh when we
                 bleed

Bill stops singing and clutches his side in pain. Lon sets his book on the ground and assists Bill.

Bill: Morgan. She's a sorceress, a witch.

Lon: Right.

Bill: I mean it! Her servants did this to me.

Lon: How?

Bill: With a dagger made of pure silver.

Lon: Silver?

Bill: It's the only thing that can kill me. The only thing that can kill any – *short pause* – monster.

Lon: What?

Bill: When the moon's full I'm almost invulnerable. Except for silver.

Lon: I'm not following this.

Bill: I'm a werewolf, Lon.

There is an ominous chord.

Lon: I'm getting you to a doctor right now.

Bill: She wants me Lon. She wants my power. She already has the three other monsters. A vampire, a ghost, and a thing with no name. She feeds from them. She uses their power. If she gets me her collection will be complete. She will have the power of all monsters. No one has ever accomplished that before. Humanity will be her slave. I got away from her servants just before she arrived. With my power she could rule the world.

Lon: You're delirious.

Bill: I'm dying.

Lon: Don't say that.

Bill: If... if she finds me here she'll take my blood. That's where the power is. I... I have to pass it on to someone else.

Lon: Like who?

Bill: It'll make you special Lon.

Lon: You're outa your mind.

Bill: You'll see the world through new eyes.

Lon: You're really sick.

Bill: Sure, you'll be different. But you'll be stronger, faster – you'll see things, smell things you never imagined.

Lon: I'm happy just the way I am.

Chorus: *(Quietly)* Come on Fate, come on, come on.

Bill: My human body's been mortally wounded. But she can only get the power when I'm the wolf.

Lon: Too weird.

Bill: There's no time!

Lon: Just a minute.

Bill: Before the moon rises!

Lon: Alright!

Pause.

Lon: What do I do?

Bill: Taste the blood.

Lon: I can't.

Bill moves to Lon, holding a bloodied finger out to him.

Bill: Just a drop on your tongue. You can do it.

Lon tastes the blood. He waits for some effect and is disappointed when nothing happens.

Lon: So now I'm supposed to turn into a werewolf whenever the moon is full?

Bill: No. You'll change whenever the moon is visible, but you'll be strongest when it's full.

Lon: And I suppose I'm gonna run around killing people.

Bill: Everything's the same when you're human – but the moon.... *Bill trails off weakly and sits.*

Lon: That doesn't sound right.

Bill: I wish I had more time to help you.

Lon: I've got to get you to a hospital.

Bill: It's okay. It doesn't hurt anymore. Be – be careful son....

Bill dies slowly. Lon holds him.

Lon: Oh Jeez. Uncle Bill. Don't be dead. *Lon moves away from Bill.* What's going on? This is all so strange. He's really dead. He's.... *Lon turns back to where Bill was lying and realizes there is no one there.* Gone. It's a dream. Just a dream.

Butch is passing the graveyard. He notices Lon and stops. Butch enters the graveyard.

Butch: Y'know... I always suspected you were a dipstick. It's just been confirmed. You okay?

Lon: I'm fine. I just – just...

Butch: You gonna puke?

Lon: Maybe. *Lon snorts suddenly.*

Butch: I'm gonna get you home.

Lon: Don't touch me!

Butch moves to help Lon. Lon grabs Butch around the throat with far more power than either of them suspect. Butch can't break the hold. After a moment Lon lets him go.

Lon: Just – just get the hell out of here!

Short pause.

Butch: Fine.

Butch exits. Lon begins to shake uncontrollably.

Lon: My head – I... I... What's happening. I hear...
something... like a voice or a song. In my head – I hear...
I hear – the moon. What's happening to me? I feel sick!

*Lon stumbles and falls behind a tombstone. As the chorus
sings, Lon's hands are seen gripping the front of the
tombstone from behind. One hand is removed and replaced
by a larger, hairy hand. The process is repeated with his
other hand. His face rises above the tombstone, contorted in
pain. He screams then disappears completely behind the
tombstone.*

Chorus: Come on fate, come on, come on
Come on fate, come on, come on
Come on fate, come on, COME ON

*There is suddenly a loud, animal roar. Lon falls onto the
ground from behind the tombstone. He lies in a very small
pile for a second then stands slowly, gradually unfolding to
reveal himself as a werewolf that is much bigger and better
built than his human form. He examines this new body in
amazement.*

NEW HAIR EVERYWHERE

Wolf: What's this I smell
What's this I feel
What's this I hear
It doesn't seem real

I feel the moon on my face
The wind in my hair
The wind in my hair
But I don't have hair there
I do have hair there
Oh God I've got –
New hair everywhere
What am I now
What have I become
I'm stronger, I'm brighter
But all this hair looks so dumb
I can smell other people
Their scent on the air
I can hear things so distant
I can't know they're there
I feel my blood pound
I feel my skin glow
I'm bursting my seams
Everything's grown
I'm stronger, I'm tougher
I have enhanced senses
Hear the world rush over rivers
And leaping tall fences
It's fantastic, amazing
I feel sparkling and fresh
I'm wearing a new body
I'm encased in strong flesh
This all might be great
But it's not really fair
To get this kind of power
And so much hair everywhere
It's not at all normal
People will stare
They'll whisper and laugh

People will stare
At all this hair
That grows everywhere
What did he do to me
It isn't fair

The werewolf quickly exits the graveyard. There is an ominous strain of music as Heidi, Shape, and Karma enter.

Shape: Aw no – he got away again.

Heidi: Wait. I sense something.

Shape: What?

Heidi: A ghostly shape. There, on the ground. Someone recently died there. Someone – magical.

Shape: Oh no! He's dead. Now what'll we do. She'll be pissed fer sure. She'll...

Heidi slaps Shape twice across the face.

Heidi: Get a grip.

Shape: What are we going to do?

Shape: Let's just run away before she gets here.

Karma: Don't be an idiot. She feeds from us. We can't escape her. We don't have enough power anymore.

The FABULOUS *chord sounds. Morgan enters.*

Morgan: Is he here?

Pause. The monsters nervously look at each other.

Morgan: My darlings, what seems to be the problem?

Shape: Well... uh... it's just that... uh... well...

Morgan: Don't waste my time Shape or I'll have to remove all your fingernails again.

Shape: He's dead!

Morgan: He's what?!

Heidi: Morgan – Dominatrix – I see his ghostly essence with my own ghostly eyes. He was there, dead.

Morgan: Where's the body?

Karma: Gone back into the ectosphere, Mistress. As it is with all monsters.

Morgan: He can't be dead.

Heidi: But he is. I told you...

Morgan: Shut up fool! I can still sense the power.

Shape: What?

Morgan: If he's dead then he's passed it on.

Karma: He wouldn't...

Morgan: He would if he knew he was dying and knew I would find him.

Heidi: But who would he pass it on to?

Morgan: Someone... someone here. In this town.

Karma: But who?

Pause. Morgan thoughtfully looks around. She sees Lon's book and picks it up. The monsters nervously look at one another, realizing they have screwed up.

Morgan: Lester High. No name inside. What a shame.

Heidi: What are you going to do?

Morgan: Visit the high school of course. We have four nights until the moon is ripe. We'll find him before that. *Morgan pulls a very long, very sharp silver dagger from a sheath beneath her cape and fondles it lovingly. The monsters smile in anticipation.* Who knows, it might even be fun.

Morgan and the monsters exit maniacally laughing. The lights change to day. We are at the high school. A number of girls enter carrying books.

LESTER HIGH

Girls: We really like to date
                   We really like to pet
                   But if he goes too far
                   I'll have to break his neck

The Brains enter led by Tod.

Brains: We really like to read
We really like to write
We really like to study
Each and every night

The Heads enter led by Liver and Muzzy.

Heads: They really like to act
Like sucks who need a life
They really like to walk
Like their asses are too tight

Brains: Go ahead and laugh
Be as cruel as you can
But you'll be digging ditches
When we're making sixty grand

Heads: Make your sixty grand. Who needs it
There's only three things that soothe my soul
They're sex and they're drugs and they're rock and
    roll
This place sucks, this school's much too dry
And they screw with your head, so you never really
    fly

The Jocks enter led by Butch and Goon. The Nerds and the Heads quickly get out of their way.

Jocks: This place's glorious, the best years of my life
I'll play a little football, and find a little wife
We really like to party, and we never ever smoke
And when we're in the shower, we never drop the
    soap

Heads: You guys are wonderful, we think you're really cool
                     And we'd like to hang with you, if you didn't drool

Jocks: Watch your mouth dropouts, you're getting on my
                     nerves
                     It wouldn't take much provocation, to get what you
                     deserve

Girls: That's right, start a fight
                     Kill each other, get it right

The kids split into their various cliques. Brent grabs Tod's binder.

Brent: Hey Tod, ya got any girly pictures in here?

Tod: Give that back.

Goon: Hey Brent, toss it here.

Tod: Come on you guys.

Brent catches the binder and opens it. Butch watches but doesn't take part in the game.

Brent: Hey, look! Comic books!

Everyone laughs. Butch takes the comics from Brent and examines them.

Butch: "The Tomb of Dracula." "The Devils' Daughter." "Werewolf by Night."

Goon: Kid stuff.

Tod: I... I like comic books.

Goon: Maybe he thinks he can fly.

Brent: Yeah. Fly.

Tod: Leave me alone.

A number of Jocks circle Tod and grab him, lifting him off the ground.

Brent: Someone keep your eye out for teachers.

Fern and Dawn enter and see what's going on. Fern breaks through the circle and confronts Brent.

Fern: Put him down!

The Jocks drop Tod. Dawn leads Tod away from then. Tod is very embarrassed.

Dawn: Come on Tod.

Goon: We're just playing around.

Fern: You guys should learn to play fair.

Brent: Hey, we're always fair.

Goon: He was readin' comic books.

Fern: What was the last book you read, Goon?

Goon: Well... uh...

Brent: *Penthouse Forum.*

Brent makes a jerking off gesture. Everyone laughs.

Goon: What makes you think you're so good?

Butch: Leave it alone. She's right.

Goon: Okay Butch.

Butch: Hey Tod, here's your comics. Sorry. We kinda bent the corners.

Tod: *Heartbroken.* Oh – oh that's alright.

Dawn: Fern, I gotta hit my locker...

Morgan enters carrying school books. Shape is dressed in black and wears sunglasses, gloves, and a hat. All stop and stare. Morgan gives them a shy smile and walks on. A long pause.

Brent: Wotta babe.

Goon: Who was that?

Stella: Where'd she come from?

Irene: What does she want here?

New Girl in Town

Jocks: Oh my god! I think I'm in love

Heads: Oh my god! I think I'm in love

Brains: Oh my god! I think I'm in love

Girls: Oh my god! I think we're in trouble

Boys: It's been the same ever since we were twelve
              All the girls we know, just like we know ourselves
              Loretta's neat and Sue's real keen
              Gloria's nifty and so is Francine
              But after a lifetime, they start to bring you down
              Praise whoever we've finally got a new girl in town
              She's hot and she's sexy
              She's fresh as the spring
              She moves like a goddess
              And she makes my ears ring
              I want to give her my heart
              I'd walk through glass on my knees
              She's a new girl like no other
              And I'm blowin' hot like a breeze

Morgan and Shape enter. Morgan carries a school timetable and a map.

Stella: Who is this girl
              This overdressed bink
              What is she pulling
              What does she think

Morgan: My name is Morgan, I'm sixteen years old
              I'm new in town, my father's dead, and I haven't any
                 friends
              We moved here from another place and I haven't any
                 friends

Tod: She's gorgeous, she's perfection
              So feminine and helpless
              She might need protection

Dawn: But I'm far too selfish
Look at her hair
So shiny and loose
Look at her hips
I feel like a moose

Morgan: I used to go to another school, but I don't anymore
I want to be a fashion model and I don't believe in
war

Butch: There's something about her that doesn't seem right
They really don't agree, her face and the light

Fern: The boys really like her, but that's what they do
The girls are all jealous because she's new

Morgan: I live with an old uncle, he's really very rich
The butler's very stuck up, and my maid's a real witch

Jocks: Welcome to Lester
We hope you'll like it here
We know you're gonna love it
It's really very dear

The Heads move in front of the Jocks.

Heads: If there's anything you need
Just give us a call
Any kind of thrill you want
We guarantee a ball.

The Brains move in front of the Pool Hall Boys.

Brains: You seem to be a cerebral girl
We're sure your marks are really great
But if they should start to suffer
Call us. No need to wait.

Morgan: Thanks so very much,
You're all too nice and kind
I think I'll like it here in Lester
Who knows what I might find.

Fern: My name's Fern.

Morgan: Hello. I'm Morgan.

Goon: Who's the big guy?

Morgan: That's my cousin. He takes care of me.

Goon: What's your name, big guy?

Shape: Shape.

Goon: Cool name.

Shape: What's your name?

Goon: Goon.

Shape: Cool name.

Morgan: Can anyone tell me how to get to classroom 30A?

Duey: I'll take your books.

Goon: I'll take your coat.

Brent: I'll drink your bath water.

Morgan: You're all so very nice. But I'd like Goon to show
me the way.

Boys: Goon?!

Melody moves to Goon and takes his arm.

Melody: Goon?

Goon: Uh... see ya later.

*Goon pulls away from Melody and takes Morgan's books.
They exit with Shape.*

Rod: Goon?

Brent: Hey, he's making time with her right now.

Doody: We can't have that.

Ferd: Let's head them off.

All Boys: Yeah.

All the boys run off after Morgan and Goon.

Irene: Can you believe that?

Stella: That girl's a mink.

Dawn: You're just jealous.

Stella: Jealous? Me? Don't be a fool. Being jealous of her
would be like being jealous of you. It doesn't make any
sense.

Fern: That's enough Stella.

Dawn: Why don't you just come out and call me a fat cow?

Stella: Because that would be rude.

Melody: Goon likes her. I could tell.

Stella: Come on girls. Let's go smoke cigarettes.

Melody: Oh yes. Let's. I love to smoke when I'm depressed.

All exit but Fern and Dawn.

Fern: She's a bitch.

FAT GIRL

Dawn:
Morning
In the morning I wake up
In the morning I wake up and look into the mirror
Sighing
I am sighing while I dress
I am sighing while I dress and look into the mirror
I brush my hair
Crying
Inside I'm crying while I brush my hair
I'm crying while I brush my hair and thinking
There's got to be another way
There's got to be a time, someday
When the pain I feel inside goes away
Someone says "you're lovely, will you stay"
Stay
I would stay.
But they don't ask you when you're fat

They never think of it if you're fat
And I hate it
I hate being a fat girl
I don't want to be a fat girl
But I have no other choice
If I did I'd give it voice
I have lovely teeth and beautiful hair
And my nails win prizes everywhere
I like my nose and I like my eyes
But they're minor assets at my size
Lonely
I get so lonely

Fern: We all get lonely

Dawn: Fat girl. Fat girl

All other girls enter led by Stella, Melody, and Irene.

Girls: Why can't we be like they want us to be
Why can't we wake up and look like they do on TV
I'd give anything for a tan and perfect smile
I'd give anything to have some sense of style

Fern: You're all over-reacting to this.

Girls: Lonely
If we were beautiful, oh if only
Then we'd never have to be lonely
We all smile, but it's phoney
We're all too heavy, or too boney

Dawn: Fat girl. Fat girl *Under the above.*

Fern: This is stupid!

Lon enters looking totally shellshocked. All the girls stare at him.

Irene: Jeez.

Melody: Is he on ludes or what?

Fern: Lon.

Lon: Oh. Hi Fern.

Fern: What's wrong?

Lon: Nothing.

Dawn: As if. That is definitely your "Something is very wrong" face.

Lon: It's sort of personal, Dawn.

Dawn: Okay, everyone else piss off. This is personal.

Stella: Come on girls, they want to be alone.

All exit but Lon, Fern, and Dawn.

Fern: You feel all right?

Lon: I've never felt better in my life.

Dawn: Actually, you've never looked better.

Fern: So what's the problem?

Pause.

Dawn: Lon?

Lon: Dawn, Fern... I... I'm not like other boys anymore.

Fern: What's that supposed to mean?

Lon: I've changed.

Fern: Changed how?

Lon: Last night...

Fern: Yes?

Dawn: What did you do?

Lon: Last night – It was horrible. It was fantastic. It was – it was...

Dawn: What did you do?

Lon: I attacked a sheep.

Fern: Why?

Lon: I wanted to kill it!

Long pause.

Dawn: No. You're not like other boys. You're bugshit crazy.

Fern: You – you killed a sheep?

Lon: No. But I wanted to. You've got to understand...

Dawn: I understand perfectly. You've become a barnyard serial killer.

Lon: No. A werewolf.

Long pause.

Fern: Are you on acid?

Lon: Look at my palm.

Fern: What?

Lon: There. A pentacle.

Fern: I've never seen that before.

Dawn: It's from beating off.

Fern: *Laughs.* Dawn!

Lon: Tonight when the moon comes out, you'll see.

Dawn: You are serious.

Lon: Meet me at the graveyard at sundown. I'll show you both.

A buzzer sounds.

Dawn: C'mon.

Fern: *To Lon.* Aren't you going to class?

Lon: Fern, I'm a werewolf.

Dawn: We're gonna be late.

Lon: At the graveyard.

Fern: Promise.

Dawn: Late.

Fern and Dawn exit.

WILL THEY BE TRUE

Lon: And when they realize just how different I am will
 they stay with me
Will they still be my friends or will they stray from me
I don't know, but I wish I knew
Will they be true
Will they be true

Morgan's house. Late afternoon. Morgan and Goon enter.

Goon: People always said this old place was haunted.

Morgan: My uncle just bought it.

Goon: Where'd Shape go?

Morgan: I sent him away so we could be alone.

Goon: Really?

Morgan: You did want to be alone with me, didn't you
 Goon?

Morgan intimately touches Goon's body. Goon gets excited.

Goon: Uh... sure.

Morgan: I thought so.

The monsters are heard off, very quietly.

Monsters: Booga booga.

Goon: What's that?

Morgan: Nothing.

Goon: Can't you turn some more lights on?

Morgan: Are you scared?

Monsters: *Off.* Booga booga.

Goon: Uh... look, I promised Melody I'd meet her...

Monsters: *Off. Louder.* Booga booga.

Goon: I'd better go. I'll catch ya later Babe.

Goon quickly begins to exit. Heidi appears in front of him.

Heidi: Booga booga.

Goon: Shit!

Goon runs in another direction. Karma appears in front of him.

Karma: Booga booga.

Goon: Ah!

Dan Riedlhuber, the Edmonton Sun

left to right – James Viveiros (Shape), Mindy Mathes (Heidi), Rick Harcourt (Goon), Juliana Pivato (Morgan in background), Clinton Carew (Count Karma).

Goon runs in another direction. Shape appears in front of him.

Goon: Not you too!

Shape: Booga booga!

The monsters grab Goon.

Goon: Let me go you freaks!

Morgan: Hold him my pets. He could be the one.

Goon: What's going on here? What have I done?

Monsters: Booga booga. Booga booga.

BE FABULOUS OR DIE

Morgan: Darling, you've done nothing wrong
You're my kind of guy, y'know
All I want is one small kiss
Don't you worry, don't you cry
It won't hurt, I promise you
Unless you have what I need
If you do I'll cut you open
And drink your blood as you bleed
If the power of the wolf
Flows through your veins
I'll smash your head on the floor
And suck up your brains
But if you're not the one
This won't hurt a bit
A quick kiss, that's it
Of course there's a price
Nothing comes free
And the price that you pay
Is submission to me
That's what'll happen
It's the cost of the kiss
I'm sure you'll enjoy it
It'll be fabulous

Monsters: Booga booga. Booga booga.

Goon: I don't want to be your – your servant.

Morgan: Don't flatter yourself darling
A servant, you'll be my slave
Now stop all this struggling
You'll gain nothing by being brave.

Goon: No!

Morgan: It's a hit you can't miss
And the price is a kiss
I guarantee you'll love it
You'll feel fabulous

Monsters: Booga booga. Booga booga.

Morgan: Be fabulous Goon, it's a great high
Kiss me, be fabulous. Be fabulous or die!

Morgan kisses Goon. A flash of light. Goon slumps to the ground.

Heidi: Well he's not the one.

Karma: Shall we eviscerate him now, Dominatrix?

The monsters lean over Goon, ready to rip him to pieces. They stand suddenly, at Morgan's command.

Morgan: No. I can use him to help me get the other boys here. How do you feel?

Goon: Fabulous.

Morgan: *Laughs.* I'll find the werewolf if I have to go through every boy in this town, one at a time!

Goon: Fabulous.

Morgan: You idiots get out there and keep your eyes open. If one of these boys was recently given the power he's probably behaving a bit oddly by now.

Heidi: What if it's not a boy? What if it's a girl?

Morgan: Don't be a fool. Go!

The monsters quickly exit. Morgan strokes Goon's hair.

Morgan: You come with me. We're going to plan a party.

Goon: Fabulous.

The graveyard. Late evening. Fern and Dawn enter.

Dawn: The graveyard? What's with your boyfriend?

Fern: He's been so withdrawn lately.

Lon enters.

Lon: You both have to leave right now!

Dawn: Say what?!

Lon: I was wrong. I never should've asked you to come.

Dawn: Mister, I'm starting to worry about you.

Lon: You've got to get out of here before the moon comes up.

Fern: I want to know what the problem is – really.

Lon: I don't want you to see me like this.

Fern: Talk to me.

Lon: Please go!

Fern: No!

Lon: The moon!

Lon retreates behind a tombstone.

Dawn: Y'know, he's almost become interesting.

Fern: Dawn, we can't joke about this. There's something wrong with him. Lon, come out of there. I'll take you home. *Pause.* Lon?

There is a moan from behind the tombstone. Long pause.

Dawn: What's happening?

The werewolf suddenly leaps out from behind the crypt. Dawn gives a small scream.

Fern: Don't move.

Dawn: What?

Fern: Look at him.

The werewolf eyes them warily.

Dawn: Fern, I'm gonna pee my pants.

Fern: Don't startle him.

Dawn: Don't startle "him?"

Fern: Lon?

Fern takes a small step toward the werewolf. It backs away from her and circles her slightly.

Fern: It's amazing.

The werewolf moves toward her slightly, sniffing.

Fern: It's magic, isn't it Lon?

Fern takes another step toward the werewolf. He growls slightly but doesn't move.

Fern: I just want to – touch your fur.

Fern reaches out to stroke the werewolf's fur. The werewolf growls and slightly jumps away, scaring Dawn.

Dawn: Fern, Jesus.

Fern: You know who I am.

The werewolf moves very close to Fern, breathing against her face and neck.

Fern: You look different. You smell different.

The werewolf touches her.

Fern: It's magic.

The werewolf suddenly pulls away from Fern, horrified and confused.

Fern: It's okay.

The werewolf exits.

Fern: Lon?

Dawn: Fern, snap out of it. He's a werewolf.

Fern: He's beautiful.

Dawn: Are you crazy?

Fern: I'm going to follow him.

Fern exits.

Dawn: Beautiful? Jeez.

Dawn exits.

A street. Late night. Fern enters.

Fern: Lon?

Spaz, Liver, and Muzzy enter from the alley.

Spaz: Whatcha doin' Fern?

Fern: Nothing?

Liver: Awful late to be doin' nothin'.

Fern: I was – was looking for Lon.

Spaz: Ain't around here.

Muzzy: Ain't no one around here.

Fern: I'd better go.

Spaz: So quick?

Liver: If you're around here this late you must be looking for something.

Fern: Let me by. I have to go.

Muzzy: Don't you wanna play?

Spaz: C'mon Fern, we ain't gonna hurtcha.

Fern: I'll scream.

Liver: *Putting his hand over Fern's mouth.* I doubt it.

There is a loud howl offstage. They stop.

Spaz: Jesus, man.

Muzzy: What was that?

Liver: A big – big dog... or something.

There is a growl from the shadows, very close. They let Fern go.

Liver: C'mon guys.

Spaz: What the hell is it?

The werewolf rises in the shadows.

Spaz: Jesus!

Muzzy: Run!

All the boys run off. The werewolf steps into the light.

Fern: Thank you.

Wolf: Stop following me.

Fern: You're beautiful.

Wolf: I'm covered with hair.

Fern: You're covered with fur. Thick, dark, beautiful fur.

Wolf: Don't come near me. I don't know what I'd do.

Fern: I can't believe you'd hurt me.

Wolf: It's different when I'm like this. I can hear things – smell things – things I shouldn't. I don't have... the control I'm used to.

Fern: Can you hear my heart beating?

Wolf: I can hear the blood moving through your veins.

Fern puts her arms around him.

Fern: Lon. It's okay.

Wolf: No – I'm different Fern. Different.

He pulls away from her.

Fern: Don't go.

Wolf: Stop following me!

The werewolf exits.

Fern: *Shakes her head sadly.* Oh Lon.

Fern exits.

A cafe. Day. All the kids enter in groups, very animated.

Butch: Has anyone seen Goon? He stayed home today.

Melody: He hasn't even called.

Fern enters.

Dawn: And he ran away?

Fern: Totally messed up.

Goon enters wearing black and looking blank.

Butch: There you are.

Brent: Goon, how ya doin'.

Goon: Fabulous.

Brent: What's with the clothes? Someone die?

Butch: Did you just say fabulous?

Melody: Goon, you didn't call me last night.

Butch: You high or something?

Melody: Goon?

Brent: I know. He's in love.

Melody: Brent!

Brent: I'd know that spaced-out look anywhere.

Melody: Goon, tell me what you think of her, really.

Goon: Fabulous.

Melody: Oh!

Irene: Don't cry, Melly.

Stella: Come on, let's go smoke.

Melody: Yes, I'd like to smoke.

Morgan enters with Shape.

Stella: Well, if it isn't little Miss Homewrecker.

Morgan: Oh Goony, there you are.

Goon: Hello Morgan.

Shape: Hi Goon.

Stella: For your information, Goon is Melody's boyfriend.

Morgan: Not anymore.

Stella: Look you –

Stella grabs Morgan. Morgan freezes. Pause.

Morgan: Take your hands off me.

Stella: Who do you think you are to walk in here –

Morgan: Shape.

Shape moves menacingly toward Stella. Stella lets go of Morgan.

Morgan: Touch me again, and you'll be very sorry.

Melody: Come on Stella. If that's the way Goon feels, she can have him.

Irene, Stella, and Melody exit.

Morgan: I came to tell you all that I'm having a party tonight.

Duey: A party!

Ferd: Terrific.

Brent: Yeah!

Morgan: It starts at eight.

Dawn: A party.

Morgan: Bring whatever and whoever you like.

Brent: We will.

Morgan: Oh yes, I almost forgot – it's a theme party.

Brent: What's the theme?

Morgan: No girls.

Pause.

Morgan: Except me.

The boys all smile.

Morgan: It's the big place on Mockingbird Hill. Starts at eight. I hope I'll see you all there.

Dawn: Hey.

Morgan: Yes?

Dawn: That's not very fair.

Morgan: No.

Morgan turns and blows a kiss at the boys as she exits with Shape and Goon.

Brent: Oh man!

Marty: This'll be great.

Barny: Are you going to go, Tod?

Tod: I'll ask, but I doubt it.

Fern: Are you guys saying that you're really going to do this?

Tod: Why not?

Fern: There's only going to be one girl there.

Brent: Yeah. But what a girl! Jesus! I've got to find something to wear.

Bruce: Me too.

Brent: C'mon guys.

All the boys exit. Butch and Tod stay behind.

Boys: Party. Party. Party. Party.

Dawn: I'd love to go to a party.

Fern: Well, we'll have our own party.

Debby: With no boys. Won't that be fun.

Charlene: I think so.

Debby: I'm going home.

Charlene: Me too.

All exit but Dawn, Fern, Butch, and Tod.

Fern: Why aren't you going?

Butch: Like you said, it's not really fair.

Dawn: Butch, you surprise me.

Butch: Sometimes I surprise myself.

Fern: Something on your mind?

Butch: What's with Goon? It was like he didn't know me or something.

Tod: Maybe Brent was right. He might be in love.

Butch: *Upset.* In love? Really?!

Tod: I don't know. I've got to go.

Butch: Me too. See you guys.

Fern: Sure.

Dawn: Ciao.

Tod: Bye Dawn.

Dawn gives Tod an indifferent wave. Butch and Tod exit.

Dawn: I never get invited to parties.

Fern: Forget the party. What about Lon?

Dawn: He's a werewolf, Fern. Were-wolf. As in, rip people's throats out.

Fern: I don't think it's really that way at all.

Dawn: Anyway, who wants to date a man with hair on his back?

Fern: Couldn't you feel the power in him?

Dawn: Yeah. Sure. But beautiful...

Fern: He saved me.

Lon enters.

Lon: Fern, I'm sorry about last night.

Fern: Don't be sorry? You were magnificent.

Lon: You can't ever tell anyone! Either of you!

Fern: But you're special.

Lon: It's a curse.

Fern: How can you say that?

Lon: How would you like to be six feet tall, two hundred pounds and covered with hair?

Dawn: The power might be worth it. Shoes would be a horror show though.

Lon: I just want to be normal again.

Fern: Look Lon, I don't know how to break this to you, but you've never been normal.

Lon: What?

Fern: You've always been too sensitive and thoughtful and kind of whiney.

Lon: Thanks a lot.

Fern: I thought you were starting to really make some progress. I was wrong.

Lon: But Fern, I'm a werewolf.

Fern: Dawn's fat and I'm a woman. We all get by.

Lon: I don't like what I become.

Fern: Just yesterday you were the one talking about magic.

Well here it is, Lon. What will you do with it?

Lon: What would you do if you were me?

Dawn: Beat the snot outa anyone who crossed me.

Fern: Enjoy it.

Lon: I don't know how.

Fern: Meet me at the graveyard tonight. We'll talk about it.

Dawn and Fern exit. After a moment Lon exits also.

Morgan's house. Night. Morgan and the monsters are there. The monsters are dressed as domestic help. The boys begin to enter in small groups.

COME

Morgan: Come on boys, step into my lair
I love the smell of your skin
And the gleam of your hair
Come in
Come
Come on children, you all look so yummy
Help yourself to some beers
There's snacks for your tummy
Come in
Come
Come on babes, don't hang back in the dark
Come admire my bod
Circle round me like sharks
Come in
Come

The boys start to party under this. The monsters circulate distributing beer and joints.

Morgan: I'm so glad you came
Please have some more
Don't worry about anything
Toss empties and butts on the floor
You sure look great
That shirt's real hot
I just love those shoes
They're new, are they not
You're so big and strong
Your hair's really fresh
I never thought I'd see you
See you here in the flesh
Have some more beer
Have some more smoke
Brush up against me
Tell me a joke

Karma: The mistress's magic works well tonight.

Shape: Yeah. They really like her.

Morgan: I'm so glad you came
It's important to me
Everything's been provided
As you can plainly see
It's all nearly perfect
But there's one thing missing
A party game to play
The kind of game that has – kissing

Barny: Kissing.

Brent: Right on.

Rod: Who're ya gonna kiss?

Morgan: Why, I'm going to kiss all of you of course.

Doody: All of us?

Morgan: Each and every one.

Brent: Wow.

Morgan:
> Now line up boys
> It's gonna be fun
> I'll kiss you all
> I'll kiss everyone

Barby: This is some crazy kind of party.

Brent: Yeah, but I'm into it.

Morgan:
> Thanks ever so for coming
> My gratitude comes with a kiss
> You'll love it. I mean it
> It'll be fabulous

Morgan begins to kiss the boys, one by one. They are transformed into zombies.

The graveyard. Night. Fern and the werewolf enter.

I SMELL YOU

Wolf: Grass and leaves
                          Wind and sky
                          Somebody singing
                          Someone saying good-bye

Fern: What else?

Wolf: I don't like doing this.

Fern: You have to. What else can you smell?

Wolf: Butterflies wings and dust in the air
                          Ozone and freon and smoke everywhere

Fern: What else?

Wolf: Exhaust fumes and perfumes and sweat
                          I smell dark things and sad things
                          And things that are wet
                          I smell anger and pain
                          I smell hunger you bet
                          I smell danger and violence
                          I smell things I don't get
                          I smell love
                          I smell loneliness
                          I smell you
                          Fern, I smell you
                          All around me
                          Clinging to me
                          Running through me
                          I smell you
                          I smell you

Fern: *Moving to him.* Is it a good smell?

Wolf: Yes.

The werewolf grabs Fern and kisses her very passionately. Fern embraces him. They sink to the ground.

Morgan's place. Night. All the boys are now entranced. Morgan is sending them out of the house.

Morgan: Go now my dark children. Find me the werewolf.

The boys exit except for Spaz, Liver, and Muzzy.

Morgan: Shape, detain those three. I saw something in their tiny minds. I'll question them further.

Shape: Yes, Dominatrix.

Shape detains Spaz, Liver, and Muzzy.

Morgan: Now my darling boys, what exactly did you see last night?

Spaz: Something dark.

Liver: Like a big dog.

Muzzy: It growled and howled.

Spaz: And hid in the fog.

Liver: We all ran away.

Morgan: Was there anyone else there?

Spaz: Fern.

Morgan: What was she doing out at that time of night?

Liver: Looking for Lon.

Morgan: Who's Lon?

Muzzy: Her boyfriend.

Morgan: How interesting.

The monsters move to the boys, staring at them hungrily.

Karma: Dominatrix, these three...

Morgan: You hunger Karma.

Heidi: It's been so long since we've had a chance to... amuse ourselves.

Morgan: Very well.

The monsters grab the boys and lead them from the room.

Heidi: Come along boys. We are going to do hideous things to you and drain you of all of your bodily fluids.

Boys: Fabulous.

The monsters lead the boys off.

Morgan: Fern's boyfriend. How interesting.

Morgan exits.

The graveyard. Very late at night. Fern is sleeping with her head in the werewolf's lap. After a moment she wakes.

Fern: I fell asleep.

Wolf: I'll walk you home.

Fern: Thank you, Lon.

Wolf: I love you, Fern.

They kiss and exit.

The school. A group of girls stand gossiping. The boys who were at the party march on, led by Goon. They chant as they move.

Boys: Nothing. Nothing. Nothing.

The girls move to the boys.

Debby: Like, what are you guys on?

Boys: We're fabulous.

Stella: You're acting like idiots.

Goon: Remember, keep your eyes open for anyone acting strange.

Melody: What was that, Goon?

Goon: Nothing.

The boys in black all exit.

Muffy: Musta been some party.

Stella: I don't even want to think about it. It makes me so mad.

Debby: There's like something weird about it all. Since when do those guys hang out together?

Dawn enters.

Dawn: How was the party?

Stella: Who cares?

Fern enters.

Fern: (*Sings*) It's a new day
It's a new age
I'm not the same girl
I've reached a new stage

Stella: At least someone's in a good mood.

Fern: I feel terrific.

Melody: Sure sure. You're boyfriend hasn't dumped you yet.

Fern: Oh Melody – don't worry. Goon'll get it together.

Stella: Easy for you to say. Your boyfriend didn't go to the party.

Fern: No. He didn't.

Dawn: That sounded satisfied.

Fern: I think my relationship with Lon has reached a new plateau.

Melody: Goody goody for you.

Fern: *To Dawn.* We're in love.

Dawn: Really?

Stella: Right. What you mean is, you love him but he hasn't
said it to you. I know this story.

Fern: You're wrong.

Dawn: What?

Irene: You mean, he said it. To you?

Fern: Yes.

Melody: That's so wonderful!

Irene: Don't cry.

Stella: Take her for a smoke.

Irene: Come on.

Melody and Irene exit.

Stella: Well what do you know, the traitor's coming back.

*Goon and Butch enter. Goon is aggressively interrogating
Butch.*

Goon: Have you had any new hair growth?

Butch: Well... yeah. Some.

Goon: Where?!

Butch: What's it to you?

Goon: Have you had any strange nocturnal experiences?

Butch: You're askin' some pretty strange questions, pal.

Goon: Where do you go when the moon is full?

Butch: Goon, what's happened to you?

Fern: Good question.

Goon: I must go.

Stella: I don't think so.

The girls surround Goon.

Stella: We want to know what's going on.

Goon: Fabulous.

Butch: Why are you asking all these questions?

Goon: Fabulous.

Dawn: Why do you keep saying fabulous?

Goon breaks through them and rushes off.

Goon: I have to go!

Lon enters.

Lon: What's wrong with Goon?

Stella: He's a dork.

184 THE WOLF PLAYS

Lon: Fern, I have to talk to you.

Stella: I bet.

Fern: Sure, Lon.

Lon and Fern move away from the others. A number of boys from each of the three groups enter, not wearing black.

Dick: Brent was asking me the stupidest questions.

Crick: And Marty's hanging out with jocks and brains.

Irene: It all started with her.

Tod: Morgan?

Ray: She seems very nice.

Stella: I don't trust her. She's different.

Fern: What's up?

Lon: About last night.

Fern: Yeah?

Debby: Haven't their parents noticed anything?

Lon: I'm sorry.

Fern: Sorry?

Butch: You kidding? Brent's dad was talking nonstop about how well behaved his son was this morning.

Fern: What do you mean sorry?

Lon: I never should've... never would've... I mean, last night... I never would've...

Fern: What?

Lon: It was the wolf. The wolf made me like that.

Fern: Are you saying last night didn't mean anything to you?

Lon: I'm saying I'm confused and last night made it worse.

Tod: Barny's parents are so high all the time they haven't even noticed.

Crick: Mebbe it's a phase or something.

Fern: I don't believe I'm hearing this.

Tod: Their recent behavior is highly deviant.

Fern: Are you saying you don't love me?

Lon: I'm saying I don't know. When I'm him everything seems so simple and straightforward. But when I turn back into me I'm as confused as ever.

Fern: You jerk!

Lon: Fern...

Fern: Get away from me Lon!

Lon exits quickly.

Dawn: Okay. So the guys are acting sorta strange. Big deal. It doesn't mean she brainwashed them or anything.

Stella: You just want to be invited to a party.

Crick: Why not? I'd go.

Tod: She might actually be doing some good if she's uniting the cliques in this town.

Butch: Not if it means she has to remove their brains to do it.

Shape and Morgan enter. Everyone stops talking.

Morgan: Hello.

Boys: Hello. Hi Morgan, etc.

Dawn: Uh – hi.

Morgan: Well – hello. It's Dawn, right?

Dawn: Right.

Morgan: Love the top.

Dawn: Thanks.

Morgan: Well, hello Fern. I didn't see you over there. How are you?

Fern: Fine.

Morgan: Really?

Fern: No.

Morgan: You look like you just lost your best friend.

Fern: I'm okay.

Morgan: Now – I'd know the look of a girl with a broken heart anywhere. Am I right?

Fern: Yes.

Morgan: Come with me. You can tell me all about it.

Fern: It's okay. I just...

Morgan: Remember, I'm new. Very objective. Come along.

Morgan leads Fern off.

Shape: Miss Morgan wants all the boys to know they are invited to a party at her place tonight.

Dawn: I don't believe it.

Shape: You may arrive anytime after eight.

Dawn: Hey!

Shape: What?

Dawn: Why doesn't she ever invite any of the girls?

Pause. Shape shrugs.

Shape: I dunno.

Shape exits.

Crick: Alright!

Ray: Let's go, Tod.

Tod: I can't, Ray. Mom and I are going to the planetarium tonight.

Ray: Too bad. See you later.

Boys: Party!

All boys but Butch exit.

Stella: They fell for it again.

Butch: There's something strange about that girl.

Debby: This is like horrible. At this rate she's going to end up being queen of the prom.

Stella: Prom? What prom? None of us will have dates.

Dawn: I'm going to that party.

Stella: Don't you have any pride?

Dawn: *Exiting.* No.

Stella: Well Butch, why aren't you going, like the other guys?

Butch: None of your business, Stella.

Tod: I wish I could go.

Stella: Girls, I think it's time we thought about putting a stop to this for good.

Charlene: Stella, I think you're right.

The girls exit.

The woods. Afternoon. Fern and Morgan are walking.

What is it About Boys?

Morgan: Come Fern, tell me all about it.

Fern:
What's been done to boys to make them need to be
    so tough
Why do they have to act as if they lack the right stuff
What is it about tenderness that frightens them off so
    quick
Why do they always chase you then resent you if you
    stick
What is it about boys
What is it about boys

Morgan:
Well you have to understand
They're complicated creatures
After all we girls got grace
And the most delicate of features
We got intuition and emotion
We're allowed to cry
We're in touch with our feelings
We survive, we always get by
They like to call it weakness
While they're having heart attacks
But if weaker we live longer
When they're stretched out on their backs

Fern:
And women can heal the pain
With tenderness it's no strain
While men are trapped in their brain
We see everything much more plain
Women will talk
Women have to talk

Both: To express themselves
To impress themselves
To free themselves
To feed themselves
By talking they share
They share everything there
By sharing they care
By caring they fare

Morgan: Better than men

Fern: Better than boys

Both: They're free

Morgan: You're free to talk to me

Fern: I'd like to, you see

Morgan: You're free, talk to me

Fern: But it doesn't seem right...

Morgan: It's about last night

Fern: About my boyfriend, Lon

Morgan: I've never met Lon

Fern: What is it about boys

Morgan: Tell me about it
Tell me about it
Trust me, I like you
Don't let this pain brew
Open the wound, let it all flow

You can't hold it in, you've got to let go
Let go

Fern: No.

Morgan: Let go.

Fern: I don't know!

Morgan: Let go!!

Fern: He said he loved me!

Morgan: Really?

Fern: And then he said he wasn't sure.

Morgan: Just like a man.

Fern: I hate him.

Morgan: Have you noticed any... changes in him lately?

Fern: Yes. Yes I have.

Morgan: What sort of changes?

Fern: He's got things on his mind!

Morgan: Why don't you tell me about them?

Fern: I don't think I should.

Morgan: *Very forceful.* Talk you little fool!

Fern: I... I have to go home now.

Morgan: Wouldn't you like to be fabulous?

Fern: No.

Fern exits quickly. Shape enters from behind a tree.

Shape: You want I should catch her, Ma'am?

Fern: No. Let's wait and see what happens tonight. She's not going anywhere.

Morgan's house. Night. Dawn enters the party dressed as a boy and hides. All the boys are now wearing black. They mill about chanting NOTHING quietly. Karma and Heidi watch them. Dawn moves to Brent.

Dawn: What the hell's going on here?

Brent: Nothing.

Dawn: Brent?!

Morgan enters with Shape.

Morgan: Is this everyone?

Goon: Everyone.

Morgan: You're wrong.

Goon: I am?

Morgan: Boys, look around you. I want to know exactly who is not here tonight.

The boys look around and mumble to one another quietly.

Goon goes and speaks to each group.

Dawn: What the hell kinda party is this?

Goon goes back to Morgan.

Goon: They say that Butch and Lon and Tod are missing.

Morgan: Go my pets. Find these three and bring them to me. Go. Go! Before the moon rises.

The boys exit. Dawn hides so Morgan and the monsters can't see her.

Karma: You'll have him tonight.

Morgan: Yes!

Heidi: Will you kill the other children after you're done?

Morgan: Of course. Now go. Help them with the search.

The monsters exit.

Dawn: I've got to find Lon!

Dawn exits.

TWILIGHT IN LESTER

CHORUS: Another night in Lester
            The sun has gone to bed
            It's twilight now in Lester
            Hear the whispers of the dead

A street. Night. Lon contemplates the moon.

Lon: No moon yet. I'm okay for a while. I should call Fern, but I'll only get messed up.

Butch enters.

Butch: Nice night.

Lon: Yeah.

Butch: Something on your mind?

Lon: Lotsa things on my mind.

Butch: Me too.

Pause.

Butch: Hey, how come you're not at the party?

Lon: What party?

Butch: Jeez, Ralston, where ya been? This new girl's been throwing these parties.

Lon: Why aren't you there?

Butch: This girl, there's something I don't like about her.

Lon: What?

Butch: I'm not sure. She seems sort of... of evil I guess.

Lon: Evil?

Butch: She's a babe. Make no mistake. But the way she looks at us – like she's looking for something – or someone.

Lon: Looking for someone?

Butch: And she's done something to all the guys.

Lon: What's her name?

Just as Butch is about to speak the sound of loud marching is heard off. Lon grabs Butch by the arm and pulls him into the graveyard and behind a tombstone.

Butch: What's wrong?

Lon: Quiet.

A number of the zombie boys enter, obviously looking for someone.

Brent: No one around here.

Barny: Shouldn't we check the graveyard?

Brent looks into the graveyard.

Brent: The graveyard is empty.

Barny: Fabulous.

The other boys follow Brent off.

Boys: We're damned. Really damned.

Lon and Butch step out from behind the tombstone.

Butch: Jesus.

Lon: Morgan!

Butch: That's right. I thought...

Lon: Who all went to this party?

Butch: Everyone.

Lon: Everyone but you and me?

Butch: Wait. Tod didn't go.

Lon: Look Butch, go get Tod and hide.

Butch: What's she doing?

Lon: She's looking for me. Only she doesn't know it's me yet. It could be you or Tod or me.

Butch: What are you talking about?

Lon: Butch, I'm a werewolf.

Pause.

Butch: That's cool.

Lon: Really?

Butch: Really.

Lon: Thanks. Now go get Tod and hide. I've got to crash that party.

Butch: I'm gone.

Lon: Good.

Butch exits.

Lon: Someone's got to warn Fern.

Dawn enters out of breath.

Dawn: Lon, I crashed this party tonight...

Lon: I know. It's my fault. Uncle Bill warned me about her.

Dawn: What?

Lon: I got so messed up I forgot all about it.

Dawn: She's a witch or something.

Lon: I'm gonna stop her.

Dawn: Even the werewolf can't stand up to her and those monsters. And what about all the guys?

Lon: She'd get my power.

Dawn: Is that what she's after?

Lon: Yes.

Dawn: Then get as far away from here as you can.

Lon: But Fern...

Dawn: I'll get Tod and Butch and we'll hole up in Fern's basement until morning. We can plan when you're normal again.

Lon: I'll get back as soon as I can.

Dawn: Go!

Lon: We have to find some way to defeat Morgan.

Dawn: How do you defeat a sorceress?

Lon: I don't know.

Dawn: Tod would know. He's into all that monster and superhero crap.

Lon: Take care of it.

Dawn exits.

Lon: The moon.

Lon runs offstage.

A street. Night. Butch enters, walking quickly. The sound of loud marching feet is heard off. Butch nervously glances around. A man enters from the darkness wearing a fedora and a large coat.

Man: Got a match?

Butch: Ah! Uh... Nope. Sorry.

Man: In a hurry?

Butch: Kind of.

Man: My, what is all that noise?

Butch: Who knows?

Man: Want to take a little walk with me?

Pause.

Butch: Walk where?

Man: Where ever you like.

Pause.

Butch: I'm sorry I can't.

Man: I'm sorry too.

Butch: Why?

Man: I thought we might be able to do this the easy way.

The man throws off his coat and hat, revealing himself as Count Karma.

Butch: Oh Jeez.

Butch turns and tries to run. Shape, Heidi, and a number of zombie boys enter. Shape grabs Butch, covering his mouth.

Shape: I'll take him back to the mistress. You guys see if you can find the other two.

Karma: Quick! Take us to the home of the little one!

The zombies lead Karma and Heidi off as Shape drags a struggling Butch into the darkness.

Tod's room. Night. Tod is lying on the bed reading a comic book. Dawn knocks on his window quietly.

Tod: Dawn?

Dawn: Let me in.

Tod opens the window.

Dawn: Where's Butch?

Tod: I don't know. What are you doing at my window?

Dawn: Look, it's not safe here. Come with me and I'll
explain on the way.

Tod: Dawn, it's after my curfew. And I'm not allowed to
have girls in my room.

Dawn: Tod, someone might be trying to kill you!

Tod: Really?

Dawn: Yes. There's stuff going on that you don't know
about. Lon's been turned into a werewolf. And
Morgan's a sorceress that wants his blood.

Tod: Lon's a werewolf?

Fern: Saw it myself.

Tod: Yowza.

Dawn: Then you believe me?

Tod: Seeing a werewolf would be excellent.

Dawn: Great. Now let's get out of here. Butch never
showed up?

Dawn: Shit. Tod, look – this sorceress – we need to know if
there's a way to kill her.

Tod: A way to kill a sorceress. That's hard. Let's see...

Tod rummages through a pile of comic books, searching for the answer.

THE WAY TO KILL A SORCERESS

Tod:

Kryptonite does Superman
It makes him really sick
Batman's only human
So a gun would do him quick
Green lantern can't fight anything yellow
And fire makes the Martian Manhunter mellow
But they're not monsters so it's really not the same
With monsters you have to learn the rules to a
    different game
Vampires are really very weak
They fear so many things
You can use a wooden stake
And other religious things
And monsters like Frankenstein
They always fear the flame
And they're never very bright
Which makes them easy game
Ghosts are harder
They have so many rules
But try a bible or a hymnal
They often fear these tools

Dawn: What about witches?

Tod:

I'm coming to that
Get off my back

Dawn: They might attack.

Tod: A sorceress is like a witch
Only she has more power
They're generally not too nice
Their disposition's often sour
They spurn religious implements
They never fall for compliments
They steal the power of others
Sometimes by being their lovers

Tod has moved progressively closer to Dawn. They are just about to kiss when Tod catches himself and pulls away from her.

Tod: But really they're only people
With magic at their disposal
You might kill them unawares
If you listen to my proposal

Dawn: What is it?!

Tod: When they're draining power from others
They can't use the power they've got
So if you caught her when she was feeding
You might give her one good shot
Yes, catch her when she's feeding
And give her one good shot

Dawn: You mean I have to wait until she's going to kill Lon?

Tod: *Nods.* Or you could always use a silver dagger.

Dawn: C'mon, let's get out of here!

Dawn grabs Tod's hand and they run off.

Morgan's house. Night. Shape enters with Butch.

Shape: This one is very strong already.

Morgan: Cute too.

Butch: Lon was right, you really are evil.

Morgan: What does Lon know about me?

Butch: *Quickly.* Nothing.

Morgan: You will cooperate, Darling.

Morgan moves to Butch to kiss him.

Butch: Don't you touch me!

Morgan: But darling, it's only a kiss. All boys love my
        kisses.

Butch: Not this one.

Butch spits in Morgan's face.

Morgan: Perhaps, you'd like a little torture to get you in the
        mood! Shape.

Shape begins slowly to twist Butch's arm behind his back.

Butch: Stop!

Stella enters.

Stella: Some party.

Morgan: You!

Stella: Where are the guys?

Morgan: Shape, get her.

Shape moves threateningly toward Stella.

Butch: Stella, run!

Stella: Hey girls!

All the girls enter from the dark. Shape withdraws.

Shape: So many

Morgan: Damn.

Stella: There's no one here.

Butch: This woman is an evil witch.

Stella: That's what I've been saying all along.

Morgan: Need I remind you ladies, you're trespassing.

Stella: You listen to me.

Stella grabs Morgan by the arm. Shape moves to protect Morgan but Butch and a number of the girls move into his path, stopping him.

Stella: There are a lot more of us than there are of you.

Morgan: Get out.

Irene: C'mon Stel. Let's go.

Charlene: Yeah.

Morgan: Have fun at the prom, girls.

Stella: You think we won't?

Morgan: It won't be much fun without escorts.

Debby: I'll have an escort.

Morgan: Really? Who?

Irene: Me.

Debby: And me.

Charlene: And me.

Melody: We'll all have escorts.

Stella: We're going to take each other to the prom.

Morgan: Sounds very amusing.

Stella: It will be. It'll be a lot of fun. At least we'll be with friends.

Morgan: Get out!

Melody: Our pleasure!

The girls and Butch exit.

Morgan: Infernal busybodies.

Karma and Heidi enter.

Karma: Has Madame aroused the natives again?

Morgan: They're no threat to me.

Karma: They are many, Morgan. A mob can be a dangerous thing.

Morgan: Enough! I am aware of the threat. Did you get the last two boys?

Heidi: No.

Morgan: Surrounded by incompetents as always!

Karma: It has been narrowed down to two.

Morgan: No. This Lon is the one.

Shape: Howja know that?

Morgan: His name has come up too may times. It can't be a coincidence.

Heidi: What are you going to do?

Morgan: The town was searched thoroughly?

Karma: Everywhere.

Morgan: Then he knows I'm on to him. We'll have to take him tomorrow night, at the prom.

Shape: I don't think he's gonna go to the prom.

Morgan: Oh yes he is.

Karma: How can you be so sure?

Morgan: Because we're going to kidnap his girlfriend.

The monsters smile with understanding and follow Morgan off.

Fern's house. The basement. Night. Fern, Dawn, and Tod are there.

Dawn: Hey Tod, wake up. We might need you to protect us.

Tod: This is boring. I'm going home.

Dawn: No.

Fern: Let him go. I hate it down here.

Dawn: But Lon said...

Fern: It's nearly daylight.

Dawn: Okay, don't blame me if you get your faces ripped off.

Tod: Hey Fern, make sure you tell Lon I want to see him when he's a werewolf.

Fern: Sure.

Dawn: Bye Tod.

Tod exits without acknowledging Dawn.

Dawn: Whoever talks to Lon first calls the other one.

Fern: Right.

Dawn: Be careful.

Fern: I'll lock everything.

Dawn exits.

Fern: Lon?

The werewolf appears somewhere else.

DISNEY

Wolf:
Fern
I can smell you, Fern
I can almost feel you, Fern

Fern:
Can you hear my thoughts with your magical senses
Do they jump over rivers, do they leap tall fences
Can you feel my love and tears all mixed together
I never want to see you again, and I'm yours forever

Wolf:
I can hear you, Fern

Fern:
I hear you, too

Wolf:
I didn't mean those things that I said
I knew what I was doing with the wolf in my head
I willing followed where my instincts were lead
But the next day I felt like I'd been hanged by a
    thread

Fern:
Who are you, Lon
Monster or man
Tell me which one
I'll accept either I can
But you have to accept them too
Before you can go very far
It's difficult I know
But accept who you are

Wolf: I get so scared

Fern: We all get scared

Wolf: Wouldn't it be perfect if life were like Disney
             I'd give anything to live in a world that's like Disney
             There's no fear, there's no pain, in that clean place
                called Disney
             And everything works out, in that place they call
                Disney

Fern: But it's not Disney, it's life
             We're all in big trouble
             You've got to come back
             We need you here on the double

Wolf: Fern, I'm afraid
             I don't know if I can
             But I want to do right
             I want to act like a man

Fern: What's a man
             Someone without doubt
             Fear or insecurity
             Someone with resolve
             And internal purity
             Lon, that kind of man
             Is sorely missed
             But that kind of person
             Just doesn't exist
             Man or woman
             We're all only human
             Teenager or werewolf
             We're all only human

Wolf: Fern, I'm on my way
            Despite the fear I feel

Both: I accept that fear
            Acknowledge that it's real
            I refuse to let it cripple me
            I'll use it as a tool
            I'll take my fear and pain
            And make them hard just like a jewel
            And put them in my heart
            And make them fuel for courage

Wolf: Fern, I'm on my way

Fern: I need you with me

Wolf: Fern, I'm on my way

Fern: We'll set Lester free

Wolf: Fern, I'm on my way

The werewolf exits quickly.

Fern: Okay little Miss "evil sorcerous who uses her beauty and charm to take over the world." Let's see how well you do against all of us.

There is a noise from the darkness.

Fern: Hello?

There is no answer. Fern walks into the shadows.

Fern: Dawn, is that you?

As Fern walks into the darkness, Karma suddenly envelopes her in his black cape.

A street. Night. The werewolf enters on a run. He stops suddenly and clutches his head.

Wolf: Fern!

Morgan appears elsewhere, now psychically connected with the werewolf.

Morgan: You should've severed the psychic connection. It led me straight to you.

Wolf: Let her go.

Morgan: How far are you from town?

Wolf: Another five miles.

Morgan: The sun will be up by the time you return.

Wolf: I'll come to your house.

Morgan: No. Let's save it for tonight. At the prom.

Wolf: Morgan –

Morgan: See you there.

Morgan's spot blinks out.

Wolf: The prom.

The restaurant. All the girls are there, as well as Butch and Tod. They whisper among themselves. Lon and Dawn enter.

Lon: She's going to make me turn into a werewolf in front of everyone.

Dawn: We'll see about that. Come on. These guys'll help out.

Lon: What if they're scared of me?

Dawn: We'll cope.

Lon and Dawn approach the others.

Lon: Hello everyone.

Tod: Lon?!

Butch: What're we gonna do?

Stella: There's some really funny stuff going on around here.

Lon: I know.

Irene: What do you know?

Lon: Look, Stella, Charlene – everyone. You've all known me for a long time...

Stella: Get on it.

Lon: I'm a werewolf.

Tod: Yow.

Long pause.

Debby: Like gross me out or what?

Lon: Not a mean werewolf – or a dangerous werewolf – but a werewolf.

Stella: You mean, we've known you all this time and you never told us you were a werewolf?

Lon: It only happened recently.

Melody: Do you get hair and fangs and everything?

Lon: Exactly.

Debby: Doubt it.

Lon: Morgan's enslaving the other guys because she's looking for me. For my werewolf power.

Charlene: A werewolf.

Charlene: Yuch!

Lon: We can beat Morgan. But we have to work together.

Debby: You're really weird, Lon.

Butch: No. Listen to him!

Irene: Butch, he's a werewolf.

Butch: So what?

Different

All (But Butch, Dawn, and Tod):
> He's different from us
> He's not the same

He can't be trusted
He should be ashamed
Why would we want
To work with someone so strange
He seems okay now
But what if he should change

Butch: But his differences could help
Could give us an advantage
A werewolf as our ally
Would up the percentage

Dawn: Everyone's different
In some special way
I'm fat, you're skinny
You're black –

Butch: I'm gay

Pause.

Lon: No way.

Tod: Really?

Dawn: There are three guys left in town. One of them's a werewolf, one's a nerd, and one's gay? Wonderful.

Butch: And if you all reject me
After so many years
You weren't worth the effort
So I won't shed any tears

Stella: Come on, girls. Let's get out of here. We'll take care of Morgan by ourselves.

Butch: I'll help you, Lon. Whatever you need
We'll back up the girls, if they don't succeed

Tod: If difference is so scary
Then I think I must report
That I'm different too
After all, I'm a dork

Dawn: Stella come on
Don't be so damn narrow-minded

Butch joins.

Look for a little mercy
In your heart, you might find it

Tod joins.

If there's anyone here
Who isn't more than we see

Lon joins.

Let that person step forward
I want to know who they might be

Lon: I'm a werewolf.

Butch: I'm gay.

Tod: I'm a dork.

Dawn: I'm fat.

Charlene: I'm black.

Stella: Skin colour doesn't count.

Charlene: It makes me different from you.

Melody: I'm gay too!

All: What?

Melody: I'm a lesibian. *Pronounced lezeebian.*

Short pause.

Dawn: Lesbian.

Melody: Whatever.

Stella: You've been going out with Goon for years.

Melody: So what? Tonight I'm a lesbian.

Debby: I'm Asian.

Butch: Step right up.

Muffy: I'm Jewish.

Tod: Join the line.

Jenny: My father's an Indian.

Lon: No problem.

Butch: That's fine.

Some Girls:

        Why should we be who they want us to be
        We end up as homogeneous as they do on TV

More Girls:

        People are people in all shapes and all types
        It's the difference that adds spice to our lives

Irene: I admit it. I'm bulemic

All: Everyone's different, in some hidden way
        Who are we to judge, who are we to say
        Everyone's different
        In some special way
        If it's positive, use it
        If it's not, send it away
        Together we can beat her
        Stella, what do you say

Stella: Don't think I'm admitting to anything by joining you. There's nothing wrong with me. I'm completely normal.

Butch: Sure Stel. No problem.

Stella: Alright. I'll do what I can.

Lon: Everyone listen up. I have a plan.

Morgan's house. Evening. The Monsters are there. Fern is tied up.

PROM NIGHT OF THE LIVING DEAD

Morgan: Look at that sky
The sun's nearly down
Another hour and we'll be
Free of this tedious town

Fern: This town is too good for you

Morgan: Yes my dear, that may be true
But you can't do anything about it

Fern: The others will all stop you

Morgan: That pack of morons, I doubt it
Oh, I can hardly wait
For your quaint little prom
Kill the werewolf, sip his blood
Raze the town, then I'm gone
I'm certain that they've got
Some useless little plan
That makes them think they can stop me
Makes them certain they can
But the plan will never work
It's true evil they lack
And I've just come too far
To think of turning back

The monsters join.

We'll break their little bones
And crush their little heads
It'll be a special Prom Night
Prom Night of the living dead
Prom Night of the living dead
Prom Night of the living dead

Morgan and the monsters exit. Shape drags Fern along.

The highschool gym. Decorated for the prom.

TOD'S VALEDICTORIAN SPEECH

Tod: Thanks every one for coming
It's nice to have you here
Forgive me if your valedictorian
Seems lacking in graduation cheer
We're here to celebrate the future
Consider new roads with unseen ends
But it's really hard to celebrate
When you're missing half your friends

Butch: Amen

Dawn: Amen

All: Amen

Tod: I can't do this.

Muffy: I miss the guys.

Lon: We'll have them back soon.

Stella: By killing the monsters? Come on.

Tod: But she won't have their power anymore. It'll be harder for her to keep everyone else under her control.

Debby: Like, I don't think this plan is going to work.

Dawn: You got a better idea?

Lon: We can do it.

Stella: This sucks.

Lon: Someone wake the band up. Let's dance.

Irene: Why do you want to dance now?

Lon: To show her we're not afraid.

Charlene: But I am afraid.

Lon: Get over it.

Jenny: How?

Lon: Dance.

Tod, Dawn, and Butch join Lon.

A Song for Lester

Tod, Lon, Butch, and Dawn:
> Let's dance
> Let's laugh
> Let's sing out
> Let's show this woman
> What Lester's about

Debby: Come on Charlene.

Charlene: Oh, alright.

Some of them begin to dance.

Tod and **Lon**: We've got the right stuff
For a town so very small

Debby: A theatre

Charlene: An ice rink

All: We even have a mall

Tod: The town is friendly
It's even quite pretty

Stella: Provided that you squint

Irene: And the streets aren't too shitty

Stella: There's nothing to do on Saturday night

Lon: When was the last time you were in on a Saturday
night

Charlene: That's right, there's always something to do

Irene: Nothing exciting, nothing that's new

Butch: You're right, That's true
But what else can you do
Until it's time to go away
Accept comfortable and stay

Lon, Butch, Tod, and **Dawn**:
If you stay appreciate the place
If you can't, then go away

Tod and **Dawn**: But in the meantime
Let's make the best of what we've got
Let's enjoy our grad
And pretend we're safe when we're really not

All: Let's dance
Let's laugh
Let's sing out
Let's show this woman
What Lester's about

Everyone starts to dance.

All: We've really got a lot
For a town so very small
A library
A roller rink
We even have a mall
Let's dance
Let's laugh
Let's sing out
Let's show this woman
What Lester's all about

Morgan enters.

Morgan: Stella, you look fabulous tonight. So do you, Irene. Melody.

Dawn: Where's Fern?

Morgan: Right here.

Morgan claps her hands. The monsters enter, supporting Fern. Everyone gasps and steps back.

Morgan: Under the care of my... friends.

Lon: Let her go!

Morgan: Ah, Lon. At last.

Lon: You're fight's with me – and no one else.

Butch: No. Her fight's with all of us.

Morgan: Anyone takes so much as a step toward me and they'll rip your girlfriend to pieces.

Stella: We'll fight you.

Tod: We'll stop you.

As Morgan speaks, Debby takes out a concealed bag filled with bibles, wooden stakes, and cigarette lighters and distributes them to the girls. Morgan and the monsters do not see her.

Morgan: Yes, I suppose you'll try. It's going to get awful bloody. Why don't we skip all the nasty stuff and get right down to it. Turn the wolfboy over to me and I'll leave this tired little town and everyone in it just as I found them.

Butch: What happens if we say take a hike?

Morgan: Then I and my... friends will kill you all.

Melody: Oh.

Morgan: I want a decision now.

Pause.

Lon: You promise you'll leave everyone else alone?

Morgan: Honest Injun.

Stella: She's lying, Lon.

Morgan: Stella, you wound me.

Stella: If she gets your power no one will be able to stop her.

Irene: That's right.

Dawn: We stick with Lon.

Morgan: Alright then.... *Morgan snaps her fingers at the monsters. They begin to molest Fern.* Let's take care of our little friend. Where should we start? It all looks so good.

Lon: Now!

All the girls reveal their various monster-fighting implements.

Morgan: What's this?!

Lon: Our way to taking care of your friends!

The girls move in three groups, attacking each monster with the appropriate item. The monsters cringe and back away. The girls form a circle around them.

Shape: Don't.

Karma: Mercy!

Heidi: Please!

Lon: Butch, get Fern.

Butch leads Fern away from Morgan and unties her.

Lon: It wasn't that hard to take care of your monsters.

Morgan: True. But you forgot something.

Lon: What?

Morgan: My other friends!!

All the zombie boys pour on from every conceivable entrance.

Dawn: Shit!

Lon: Run!

The girls attempt to flee the stage, but the boys catch and detain them all. It is absolute pandemonium.

Melody: Goon, let me go!

Butch: Guys, we're your friends.

Everyone onstage who isn't entranced is paired with someone who is.

YOU'RE MY FRIENDS (IF I SAY SO)

Morgan: You thought you were smart
Thought that you could play tricks
But everything has proven –

Butch: We're all stupid dicks

Morgan: They'd crush your empty heads
Follow me to this planet's ends
I've got nothing but their devotion
After all, they're my – friends

Dawn: They're not your friends! If they weren't messed up they'd have nothing to do with you.

Morgan: You're wrong.

Morgan gestures magically. The kids' bodies are jolted.

Tod: Oh God! She's taken control of our bodies!

As Morgan sings she leads the kids in an unwilling and grotesque disco routine.

Morgan: They're my friends
If I say so
They're my friends
Unless I say no
Everyone's my friend
Or it's no go
Cuz I say so
Unless I say no
But I won't be selfish
They're your friends too
Why don't you all dance
Before we are through

Dance to my song
As the moon rises
Say farewell to your friends
Until he werewolf-izes

Lon, Tod, Butch, and Fern are held back by a number of other boys.

Lon: Morgan, you're sick! Let them go!

Morgan: Please don't be upset, but I have to say no.

Lon: Let me go!

The monsters join Morgan. The boys and girls dance. Tod, Butch, and Lon struggle with their captors, but cannot get away. The dance turns into a mad waltz.

Morgan:

You're my friends
If I say so
You're my friends
Unless I say no

Girls:

We'll never do your bidding
We mean it
Don't think we're kidding
We're serious
We mean it

Boys:

We think it's great
We think it's swell
We really love
Prom Night hell
Prom Night hell

Morgan: You're my friends
All of you
Everyone

Fern: Lon, get out of here. You have to.

Morgan: We'll dance until moon time
We'll entertain ourselves
A little bit
We'll dance until Armageddon
You'll all witness it

Girls: We're not your friends

Morgan: For eternity
It never ends

Boys: Children of the Damned

Fern: Lon, the moon

Tod: He's gonna do it?

Lon: Not yet. But soon
I'll fight it
I'll fight it

Butch: We're not your friends

Boys: Prom Night of the living dead

Monsters and Morgan:
You're my (her) friends
Don't fight it
Don't push it
There's nothing to do

Morgan:	You're my friends (*Overlapping*)
	If I want you
	I can taunt you
	I will haunt you

Monsters:	We will hunt you
	If we want you
	And we want you

Fern: The moon!

Morgan: The moon!

Lon: The moon!

All stop dancing. Everyone watches Lon.

MOON TIME

Morgan:	Moonlight
	Dream time
	Into an inky sky
	Watch her climb
	The hour of the wolf
	Listen to the clock chime
	It's time

Lon:	It's time

Fern:	Time

Tod/Fern:	Time

Lon: You can have anything you want. Just let the others go.

Morgan: I'll have everything I want anyway.

Lon: Fern, I'm sorry. I tried.

Heidi: Look, here it comes.

Shape: Through the skylight.

Karma: Thus starts the rule of eternal twilight!

Lon: No!!!

Lon suddenly breaks free of the boys restraining him.

Morgan: Surround him quick. He can't get away.

Lon: Goon – guys. I don't want to hurt you.

Dawn: What can we do?

Lon: Get out of my way.

Morgan: Now, as the first touch of moonlight caresses his brow.

Lon: Stay away!

Morgan: Now!

Lon begins to contort as the moonlight strikes him and the change comes upon him. A deluge of boys piles on top of Lon, burying him completely.

Fern: Lon?!

Dawn: Let him go!

Butch: Lon?

Morgan: More. More. Get him!

More boys run at the werewolf.

Morgan: *To monsters.* Incompetents, help them!

The monsters move into the fray. All the boys join the fray. The boys holding Tod, Fern, and Butch let them go as they enter the fight.

Dawn: We've got to do something!

Tod: The monsters! They're the strongest!

Butch: The monsters?

Tod: If she doesn't have their power she won't be able to control the guys.

ROUGH GIRLS

Dawn:
Girls, girls
Reclaim your stuff
Let's show these monsters
That we can play rough

The girls reclaim their anti-monster implements.

Stella: Kick off your shoes

Irene: Hike up your dress

Dawn: Prepare to get dirty

Fern: We'll leave here a mess

With a howl the werewolf leaps through the pile of boys .

Girls: Get them now!

*The girls charge into the fray, basically attacking the
monsters, but also the boys. Worried, Morgan flees to the
sidelines and screams at the boys and her monsters.*

Girls: Now we'll be whoever we need to be
                     Now we'll break through the lies of TV
                     Now we'll do what needs to be done
                     Keep those monsters from Lon, block every one

Boys: Nothing in our heads
                     Nothing. Nothing
                     Nothing in our hearts
                     Nothing. Nothing

Karma: Mistress they are too many.

Morgan: Fight them you fools!

Shape: Too many.

Morgan: They're only mortals!

Heidi: A mob of mortals.

*A group of the girls separate the monsters from the boys. The
monsters are trapped and helpless. Morgan, working to
retain control of the monsters, lets her attention wander from
the zombies. The zombies wander aimlessly. Butch, Lon,
and Tod herd them into a corner and keep them there .*

Girls: Back. Get back
You're not so smart
We'll give you fire, a bible
A stake through the heart
Fire, a bible, a stake through the heart

*The above line is repeated until the monsters are dead.
Morgan rushes forward to intervene. A group of girls blocks
her.*

Morgan: My monsters! My precious monsters!

Shape: Morgan, help us!

Morgan: Let me through! If they die their power is lost to
me!

Dawn: That's the whole idea!

Heidi: *Screaming.* Stop! Stop!

Shape: Morgan –

*Shape, Heidi, and Count Karma die. They writhe and smoke
and dissolve.*

Irene: Jeez!

Tod: Yow!

Morgan: My monsters.

Tod: Quick! Her power should be very low.

Melody: The guys are still zombies.

Butch: Get her!

Morgan suddenly grabs Melody. Morgan pulls a silver dagger from beneath her cloak and holds it at Melody's throat.

Morgan: You didn't really think I'd walk into this unarmed, did you?

Stella: Let her go.

Morgan: I'll slit her throat wide open. I mean it.

The girls all stop. Morgan gestures to the boys.

Morgan: Hold them!

The boys take the girls captive. Each of the girls is disarmed. Morgan pushes Melody away and Goon holds her.

Morgan: Do you have any idea what you have cost me, you foolish girls?

Dawn: That was the idea.

Morgan: I'll have to find three other monsters now.

Fern: Good.

Morgan: Oh well, at least I'm starting out with a werewolf. Isn't that right, Lon?

The werewolf steps forward.

Wolf: Yes.

Butch: Don't.

Morgan: You don't want anything horrible to happen to all these lovely young ladies now, do you?

Butch: We can take her, Lon.

Wolf: Not while she's still commanding the guys.

Dawn: You can't –

Wolf: She'll only get my power now. It's not enough for what she wants.

Morgan: But it's a start.

Wolf: You have to promise to leave here.

Morgan: I don't have to promise anything. Now get on your knees.

The werewolf goes to his knees. Morgan moves behind him, brandishing the knife.

Wolf: She won't be very strong. There are enough of you to drive her away.

Stella: What about the guys?

MORGAN'S MISTAKE

Morgan: They remain mine
I keep them in bliss
They live for my kiss
To remain fabulous

Dawn: Kiss?

Wolf: Promise you'll free them or I'll fight you, Morgan. To the death.

Morgan: Oh alright – I promise.

Morgan pulls the werewolf's head back, baring his throat. She raises the knife. The girls try to move forward, but the guys block them.

Stella: Let us go.

Butch: Kiss the boys!

Loretta: What?

Morgan: What are you doing?

Butch grabs Brent and kisses him, just as Morgan is about to bring the knife down. Brent snaps out of his daze.

Brent: What's happening?

Dawn: Kiss them!

The girls kiss the boys. The boys are freed. Morgan moves toward them.

Morgan: Stop that.

Goon: Hey!

Barny: We're free.

Morgan: You'll all pay for this.

The werewolf stands, turning.

Wolf: You freed them.

Fern: We're not your hostages anymore.

Fern: Lon!

Wolf: Fern!

The werewolf turns his back to Morgan to greet Fern who is moving toward him. Morgan grabs the werewolf and draws the blade across his throat. Fern screams. There is a great deal of blood.

Morgan: The power is mine!

The werewolf falls into Fern's arms.

Fern: Lon?!

Dawn: The power!

Morgan holds the blood covered dagger aloft. She runs her finger over the blade, catching the blood on her finger.

Morgan: The blood! I will feed!

Stella: No!

Butch: Stop her!

Tod: The power!

Stella grabs Morgan's hand to keep her from tasting the blood. They grapple. The dagger falls clear of them.

Morgan: Let me go!

Stella: Never!

Morgan: I must feed.

The lights become more erratic. Dawn grabs the knife.

Morgan: Let go of that knife!

Morgan is still trying to reach the blood on her hand with her mouth. Stella attempts to restrain her, with little success.

Tod: Don't let her taste the blood!

Stella: Help me!

The others move forward to help Stella just as Morgan twists away from her. Morgan quickly licks the blood from her hand.

Butch: No!

Tod: She drank it.

Morgan: Nothing's happening? What's wrong!

There is a loud growl from the back of the gym. The kids part and Dawn enters from behind them. She has been transformed into a she-wolf who is even bigger than Dawn.

She-wolf: You're two seconds too late.

Morgan: You!?

She-wolf: Call me She-wolf.

Tod: Awesome.

Morgan: I will have that power!

Brent: Stop her!

Stella: Keep her away from Dawn!

*Morgan gestures magically. The lights flicker and go wild.
There is lightning and the sound of thunder and a loud wind.
The kids attempt to get to Morgan but discover she is
protected by a force field.*

Tod: Of course. A force field!

Morgan: I'm coming for you girl.

Stella: Everyone! Stay between her and Dawn.

She-wolf: No. I'll take her on.

Morgan: Come on in.

*Dawn hands the knife to Stella and steps through the force
field, motioning the others to stay back.*

She-wolf: Okay, let's do it!

Morgan: You're out of your league, Dawn. Most men can't
handle the power, let alone a girl.

She-wolf: Girl this bitch!

Dawn punches Morgan in the face.

Morgan: You're dead!

She-wolf: Come on then!

Dawn leaps at Morgan. They grapple and fall to the ground.

Morgan: Let me go!

She-wolf: Fat chance.

Morgan: I'll kill you

Tod: The force field

Stella: It's breaking up.

Tod: She can't concentrate when she's fighting.

Morgan: Abomination!

She-wolf: Cowbitch!

Butch: Let's go!

Stella moves toward Morgan uncertainly, holding the dagger.

Morgan: Bleed you fat pig!

She-wolf: Screw you.

The kids surround the she-wolf and Morgan. Some of the boys attempt to pull Morgan from the she-wolf.

Butch: Get her off.

Morgan: Yes! Bleed!

Tod: Stella!

Stella: I can't.

Tod: She's killing Dawn.

Butch: Stel!

Stella raises the dagger and plunges it into Morgan's back. Morgan screams and gets off the she-wolf. She tries to reach the knife in her back.

Morgan: No! No!

MORGAN'S DEATH

Morgan: You've killed me
You've killed me
You've killed me
You've killed me

Morgan dies. Her body dissolves into smoke as the kids watch, thunderstruck.

Butch: You – we did it.

Brent goes to Stella and holds her.

Brent: You okay?

Stella: I'll live.

Melody: Goon?

Goon: Melody. Honey.

Goon moves to Melody to embrace her. She pulls away.

Melody: Sorry. I'm a lesibian now.

Goon: Really? What's a lesibian.

Barny: What's been going on?

She-wolf: It's a long story.

Doody: Jeez Dawn, you're a werewolf.

She-wolf: And Butch's gay and Tod's a dork and Lon was a werewolf.

Brent: Shit.

Tod: Isn't she astounding.

Stella: Don't worry. We'll try to find a way to change you back.

She-wolf: Get a life, Stella. Who wants to change back?

Debby: But what'll you do?

She-wolf: Whatever I want to.

Tod: Dawn. I – I think you're very pretty.

She-wolf: Tod, c'm 'ere.

Tod goes to Dawn. She grabs him and kisses him passionately.

She-wolf: I think you're very pretty too.

Tod: Wow!

Fern: Lon.

She-wolf: Lon!

The kids scatter revealing Fern holding Lon's now human body. There is no blood on the body.

She-wolf: Fern?...

FERN'S LAMENT

Fern:

Oh, I wish he was here
Oh, I wish he was with me
Oh, I wish he were warm
I wish I ould be
Where ever he is

She-wolf: Wait!

Irene: What?

She-wolf: Who says that whatever happened to him as a werewolf has to happen to him as a person.

Charlene: I don't get it.

She-wolf: They're different beings. What happens to one physically might not necessarily happen to the other. Look, there's none of the wolf's blood on him.

Stella: He's not breathing, Dawn.

She-wolf: Come on guys, think about what just happened here. Magic. We've seen it.

Fern: There's no magic in Lester.

Irene: Yes there is.

Melody: There was enough magic to beat Morgan.

She-wolf: Fern, let me try. Let's all try.

Fern nods and rises. The she-wolf sits and holds Lon's head.

Tod: Well?

She-wolf: I don't know. Give me a minute. I can sense something deep inside of him.

I SENSE A SPARK

She-wolf:
I sense a spark
A lost germ of light
I feel some warmth
But it's lost in the night
Can you hear me, Lon
Can you feel me, Lon
Can you feel this power
I'm sending to you
Follow it, Lon
You know what to do

Fern: Lon?

Stella: Come back.

Butch: Lon.

She-wolf: Yes! Something's happening. Keep calling him.

Melody: Lon!

Tod: Lon!

Girls: Come back, Lon
Come back to Lester

Boys: Come back, Lon
Come back to Lester

She-wolf: The light's growing brighter
I can feel it coming closer

Fern: Lon, you feel my love
I'm sending it all out
Lon, you feel my love
As loud as a shout

All: Lon, you feel our friendship
We need you with us
Come back to Lester now
Before it's too late
Come back to Lester
Come meet your fate
Come back to Lester
Before it's too late
Come back

Fern: Before it's too late

All: Come back, Lon
Come back
Come back

Pause. All wait expectantly. After a moment, when nothing happens they turn away, very sad. Only Tod and the she-wolf are left at the body.

Tod: It was a good idea.

She-wolf: Yeah. Right.

Tod: Hey, you're bleeding.

She-wolf: Where?

Tod: On your neck.

She-wolf: The witch cut me.

Tod takes a bit of the blood on the she-wolf's neck on his finger and runs it along Lon's lips. They watch Lon carefully.

Tod: Check it out!

She-wolf: Yes. Yes!

The other kids move back to Lon's body. Lon opens his eyes. Everyone cheers.

Lon: I'm alive. Alive! It was so cold – so dark.

She-wolf: Hiya.

Lon: You got the power.

She-wolf: You betcha.

Lon: You don't mind?

She-wolf: I love it!

Lon: It's so good to be back.

Fern: Lon.

Lon: Fern.

Lon and Fern embrace.

Fern: I'm so glad.

Lon: It's so good to see you. It's so good to see everyone.

IT'S GOOD TO BE ALIVE

Butch:
It's good to be alive
No matter who or what you are
It's good to be living
Whether you're here or far

Lon:
It's good to feel warmth
And see familiar faces

Tod:
It's good to be at home
And dream of exotic places

She-wolf:
It's good to be fat
It's good to be boney
It's good to be popular
It's good to be lonely
As long as you're alive

Stella/Fern:
It's good to be alive
Most anywhere
It's good to be alive

She-wolf: Even though I'm covered with hair

Stella: Even though you're covered with hair

All: It's good to share
It's good to care

Girls: It's good to know
Life never comes late

Boys: It's good to learn
It's not all up to fate

Fern: It doesn't control us
It's not all that hot
I defy fate to make anyone into
Something they're not

All: It's a new day
It's a new age

She-wolf: I've got a new body

Lon: We've reached a new stage

Boys: So come on Fate
We're ready for you
We'll use you to advantage
We've learned something new

Girls: Come on Fate
We're ready to fight
We'll decide for ourselves
What's wrong and what's right

All: Starting tonight
We're ready to fight
Come on Fate
We're ready to fight

We'll decide for ourselves
What's wrong and what's right
Starting tonight
The future's in sight
So come on Fate, come on, come on
Come on Fate, You're already late
Come on Fate, come on come on
Feel my need don't hesitate
Come on Fate, come on come on
Come on Fate, come on, come on, come on, come
   on, COME ON!

Blackout.

BIOGRAPHY

Playwright Brad Fraser, born in Edmonton in 1959, began winning Alberta Culture Playwriting competitions when he was a 17 year old student in theatre arts at Victoria Composite High School. For two summers he attended the Banff Centre Playwrights' Colony, headed by Sharon Pollock. He wrote and directed his first staged play, *Mutants*, solicited for the 1980-81 season by Walterdale Theatre Associates, Edmonton's community theatre, where he was also an actor, set designer, and stage manager. The following season, 25th Street Theatre, Saskatoon premièred *Wolfboy*, with further productions at Theatre Network, Edmonton; Touchstone Theatre, Vancouver; and Theatre Passe Muraille, Toronto. Two other works were performed at Passe Muraille: *Rude Noises (for a Blank Generation)*, a collective creation with Paul Thompson in 1982, and *Young Art* in 1986. Fraser subsequently wrote *Chainsaw Love* (1985) and *The Return of the Bride* (1988) for the Edmonton Fringe Festival.

In 1986, Fraser became resident playwright at Edmonton's Workshop West Theatre. Here he began working on *Unidentified Human Remains and the True Nature of Love*, premièred in Calgary at Alberta Theatre Projects' playRites 1989. With this play Fraser achieved national and international recognition with productions in Toronto, Edmonton, Montreal, Chicago, New York, Milan, Edinburgh, London, and Tokyo. The movie version, adapted by the playwright and directed by Denys Arcand, was released in 1993. For three seasons Fraser wrote and/or directed plays for the Edmonton Teen Festival at the Citadel Theatre: Jeffrey Hirschfield's *Blood Brothers* (1989); a revised *Young Art* (1990); and *Prom Night of the Living Dead*, with music by Darrin Hagen (1991). Release of a film version of *Prom Night* is pending. *The Ugly Man* was premièred at playRites 1992 with subsequent productions in Montreal and Edmonton. The French version, (*L'homme laid*), directed by Derek Goldby at Théâtre de Quat'Sous, was published in spring 1993. The French translation of *Human Remains (Des restes humains non-identifiés et la véritable nature de l'amour)* is scheduled for publication in fall 1993.

Fraser's most recent work includes a musical version of the Craig Russell movie, *Outrageous*, in collaboration with Darrin Hagen and Andy Northrup, and a play, *Poor Superman*, to be produced in Cincinnati in winter 1994.